**BY SOPHIE KAY
AND THE EDITORS OF CONSUMER GUIDE®**

THE CHICKEN COOKBOOK

FAWCETT COLUMBINE ● NEW YORK

CONTENTS

Published by Fawcett Columbine Books, a unit of CBS Publications, the Consumer Publishing Division of CBS Inc.

First Fawcett Columbine printing: May 1981
10 9 8 7 6 5 4 3 2 1
Printed in the United States of America

Library of Congress Catalog Card Number: 80-85363
ISBN: 0-449-90049-5

Food Styling for Photography: Gail Klatt
Color Photography: Dave Jordano Photography Inc.
Cover Design: Frank Peiler

About the Author: Sophie Kay is a nationally prominent home economist and the author of eight cookbooks, including PASTA COOKERY and YOGURT COOKERY. A graduate of Northwestern University with a degree in home economics and journalism, she has held a variety of positions in the field of home economics and has conducted numerous cooking schools across the country. For over 10 years, the Milwaukee, Wisconsin, resident has conducted a bi-weekly cooking segment on a popular television program in that city. Prior to that, she was the hostess/emcee of a daily television cooking program in Chicago, Illinois.

CONTENTS

Introduction

Chicken is a mainstay in the American diet. It has universal taste appeal; it's widely available, economical and high in protein yet relatively low in calories.

Chicken is also remarkably versatile. It lends itself to almost every type of cooking: roasting, baking, frying, sautéing, braising, stewing, poaching, broiling and grilling. It can be prepared whole, cut into pieces, chopped, shredded or ground.

The popularity of chicken is international; many countries include famous chicken dishes in their cuisines. The French, for example, combine chicken with wine in Coq au Vin; Italians pair it with tomatoes in Chicken Cacciatore; Russians bone and fill it in Chicken Kiev; Japanese slice and stir-fry it in Sukiyaki.

Nutrition

Chicken is an excellent source of high-quality, complete protein and contains the amino acids essential to build, maintain and repair body tissues. It also contributes significant amounts of Vitamin A, niacin, riboflavin, thiamine and iron.

Compared to many protein-rich foods, chicken is low in calorie count and fat content. For instance, the edible portion of an uncooked 3½-ounce (100 g) serving of a broiling/frying chicken contains about 150 calories and about 21 grams of protein.

Types of Chicken

The age and weight of a chicken at the time it is killed determines how it will be classified for marketing as well as the kind of cooking method intended for it. Generally, young birds are more tender and lighter in flavor than older ones. The young birds are best for broiling, frying, roasting and sautéing. Older chickens are better suited to longer cooking methods to tenderize their meat and develop their full, rich flavor.

Types of chicken available include:

Broiling/frying Chickens. Also called "broilers," "fryers" or "broiler/fryers," these chickens are 7 to 9 weeks old and range in size from about 1½ to 3½ pounds (675 to 1600 g). They are very tender, mildly flavored and can be broiled, fried or roasted.

Roasting Chickens. Also called "roasters," these birds are about 16 weeks old and usually weigh between 4 and 6 pounds (1800 and 2700 g). They are tender and are excellent for roasting but also can be fried or broiled.

Capons. These are male chickens that have been castrated. They are approximately 16 weeks old and generally range in size from 5 to 7 pounds (2250 to 3150 g). They are meatier, more tender and flavorful and contain more fat than roasting chickens. They are excellent for roasting.

Stewing Hens. Also called "heavy fowl," "soup chickens" or "boiling hens," these adult chickens range in age from 1 to 1½ years and in size from about 4½ to 7 pounds (2 kg to 3150 g). Their meat is richly flavored but tough and stringy, so they must be cooked by a moist-heat method. That's why they're ideal for soups and stews.

Rock Cornish (Game) Hens. These birds are usually 4 to 6 weeks old and range in size from ¾ to 2 pounds (340 to 900 g). They are very tender and mildly flavored. They can be roasted, broiled or fried.

How Chicken Is Packaged

Ready-to-cook chicken is marketed in a variety of ways and generally is packaged in clear plastic bags or on heat-sealed, plastic-wrapped, disposable trays. Some of the packs available include:

Whole Chicken. All types of chicken (broiling/frying chickens, roasting chickens, capons and stewing hens) are available in the whole, uncut form. Usually the neck and giblets (heart, liver and gizzard) are wrapped separately and packed inside the bird.

Cut-Up Chicken. This is the complete chicken (usually with giblets) that has been cut into serving-size pieces. Broiling/frying chickens usually are the only birds marketed this way.

Chicken Halves or Quarters. Smaller broiling/frying chickens (usually 1½ to 2½ pounds or 675 to 1125 g) are marketed this way. Halves are obtained by cutting the chicken lengthwise down the center. Quarters are obtained by cutting the bird into four pieces: two breast halves with wings attached and two whole legs (thigh and drumstick attached).

Chicken Legs. These are whole legs (thigh and drumstick attached) from broiling/frying chickens.

Chicken Thighs. These are thighs from broiling/frying chickens that have been separated from the drumsticks.

Chicken Drumsticks. These are drumsticks from broiling/frying chickens that have been separated from the thighs.

Chicken Breasts. The breasts from broiling/frying chickens often are packaged separately. The breasts can be whole (with bones) or split into halves.

Boneless Chicken Breasts, Chicken Cutlets or Chicken Supremes. The names may differ, but the cut is the same: halves of breasts from broiling/frying chickens that have had all of the bones removed.

Chicken Wings. These are wings that have been removed from the birds, which usually are broiling/frying chickens.

Ground Chicken. This item is available in some parts of the country. It is boneless, uncooked chicken, usually from broiling/frying chickens, that can contain both white and dark meat.

Chicken Livers. Livers could come from any kind of chicken, but usually they are derived from broiling/frying chickens.

Miscellaneous Items. Chicken also can be processed into assorted products such as frankfurters, luncheon loaves, bologna, smoked or canned cooked chicken.

Selecting Chicken

Although packages are not always marked with an inspection stamp, virtually all chickens sold in this country have been inspected for wholesomeness. Inspection is done either by the United States Department of Agriculture or by individual state systems which have standards equal to those of the federal government.

Chicken is also graded. Most of the ready-to-cook chicken that's available for retail sale is U.S.D.A. Grade "A." There are Grades "B" and "C," too, but they rarely are found in stores.

Whether buying chicken whole or cut into pieces, select ones that have clear skin without bruises, blemishes or pin feathers. On broiling/frying and roasting chickens, the skin should be soft and thin; on stewing hens it will be thick.

Skin color can vary from creamy white to deep yellow. Contrary to what some people may think, the color of a chicken's skin is not an indication of quality,

flavor or nutritional value. It merely reflects what the chicken was fed.

An appropriate fat covering under the skin is desirable. Roasting chickens and capons should have a well distributed layer of fat. Broiling/frying chickens should have a moderate fat covering, while stewing hens will have little.

The cartilage at the tip of the breastbone can provide an indication of a chicken's age. On young birds, such as broiling/frying chickens, the cartilage will be flexible, on older birds, such as stewing hens, it will be firm.

In many parts of the country, chicken is being open-dated, which means that the last date upon which the chicken should be sold is stamped on the package. If the package is not dated, look for visual signs of freshness. The chicken should be firm and moist-looking with good color; avoid any meat that is gray or pasty-looking. Also, don't select any packages that were not sealed properly or that have been punctured.

If you notice a strong, unpleasant odor when you first open a package of chicken, it doesn't necessarily mean that the meat has spoiled. Occasionally an odor will develop because of oxidation inside the package. When this happens, the odor will disappear within a few minutes after opening the package. If the odor does not disappear, return the chicken in its original package to the store for a refund or replacement.

If you are interested in saving money, compare prices when you shop for chicken. Generally whole broiling/frying chickens are priced less per pound than cut-up chicken parts. Stores frequently feature specials on broiling/frying chickens; watch for them and take advantage of them when they occur. Also, larger birds yield a greater proportion of meat to bone, which means more value for the money.

When you're cutting up or boning chicken, don't discard any parts of the bird. Backs, necks, giblets and bones from uncooked chickens should be saved for preparing broth or soup.

Amount of Chicken to Purchase

The amount of chicken needed for each serving will depend upon how it's cooked and how hungry people are. As a general rule, allow about ½ pound (225 g) of uncooked chicken with bones per serving. After cooking, this will yield about 3 ounces (85 g) of edible meat without bone.

For cut-up chicken, figure one serving to be one whole leg, two drumsticks, two thighs, one breast half or four wings.

For ground uncooked chicken, allow 4 to 5 ounces (115 to 140 g) per serving.

INTRODUCTION

For Rock Cornish Hens, plan one serving for each small bird (about 1 pound or 450 g). The larger birds (1½ to 2 pounds or 675 to 900 g) will usually yield two servings.

When chopped cooked chicken or ground uncooked chicken is required as an ingredient in a recipe, it is sometimes difficult to judge how much chicken should be purchased. The following information can be used for guidelines:

Kind of Chicken	Approximate Yield
Two whole chicken breasts (about 10 ounces or 285 g each)	2 cups (500 mL) chopped cooked chicken
One broiling/frying chicken (about 3 pounds or 1350 g)	2½ cups (625 mL) chopped cooked chicken OR 3 cups (750 mL) ground uncooked boneless chicken
One stewing hen (about 5½ pounds or 2475 g)	5 cups (1250 mL) chopped cooked chicken

Storing Chicken

Fresh, uncooked chicken can be kept up to two days in the refrigerator. If you are not certain it will be cooked within that time, it should be frozen as soon as it is brought home from the store.

Chicken that has been packed in plastic bags or on trays and heat-sealed in plastic may be kept in the refrigerator in the original packaging. Chicken that has been wrapped in meat market paper should be removed from its original paper, rinsed with cold water and repackaged in plastic bags, clear plastic wrap or food storage containers before refrigerating.

All refrigerated fresh chicken should be kept in the coldest part of the refrigerator and used within two days.

For freezing, chicken should never be allowed to remain in its original store packaging. When it's brought home from the store, it should be repackaged immediately. The best materials to use for wrapping chicken are those that are moisture-proof and vapor-proof. These include specially coated freezer paper, freezer bags and heavy-duty aluminum foil.

To prepare whole uncooked chickens for freezing, remove the giblets from the body cavity, rinse the chicken with cold water and pat dry with paper toweling. Trim off any excess fat. Wrap the chicken in moisture-proof, vapor-proof material, label it with the date and freeze. Wrap, date and freeze the giblets

Maximum Storage Time at 0°F (−18°C) for Freezing Chicken	
Whole chicken, uncooked (home frozen)	8 to 12 months
Whole chicken, uncooked (comercially frozen)	12 months
Cut-up whole chicken and chicken parts, uncooked	6 to 9 months
Giblets, uncooked	3 months
Cooked chicken, in gravy or broth	6 months
Cooked chicken, without gravy or broth	1 month
Cooked chicken, in main dishes or casseroles	3 to 6 months
Cooked chicken, fried or roasted (without stuffing)	1 month

separately. The same procedure should be followed to freeze chicken parts, but they should be packed a few pieces to a package so they freeze quickly.

Cooked chicken can be refrigerated up to two days. It should be cooled slightly after cooking, wrapped in plastic wrap or placed in food storage containers. Stuffing should be removed from the chicken, wrapped and stored separately in the refrigerator.

If packaged properly in moisture-proof, vapor-proof material, cooked chicken can be frozen but there may be some loss in its quality and flavor. Chicken that has been stuffed should be separated from its stuffing before freezing. The stuffing should not be frozen.

Thawing Frozen Chicken

The best way to preserve quality when defrosting uncooked frozen chicken is to thaw it gradually in the refrigerator. Allow enough time for the bird to thaw completely. A 1 to 2 pound (450 to 900 g) bird will take about 12 hours; a 2 to 4 pound (900 to 1800 g) bird will take 12 to 24 hours; a 4 to 6 pound (1800 to 2700 g) bird will take 24 to 36 hours.

For faster defrosting, chicken can be thawed by the cold water method. Place the frozen bird, in its original freezer-wrapping material, in a large pan or the sink and cover completely with cold water. Change the water frequently and let thaw until the chicken feels pliable but still cold. A 1 to 2 pound (450 to 900 g) bird will take about 1 hour; a 2 to 3 pound (900 to 1350 g) bird will take 1 to 2 hours; a 4 to 6 pound (1800 to 2700 g) bird will take 3 to 4 hours.

Chicken should be cooked immediately after it is thawed. It should never be refrozen.

Testing for Doneness

There are several ways of testing a cooking chicken to see when it is done. The most accurate method is to use a meat thermometer. Before putting the chicken into the oven, the thermometer should be placed in either of two places: the center of the thigh meat away from any bones or in the center of the body cavity if the bird has been stuffed (see photographs in Preparation Techniques). When the thermometer inserted into the thigh registers 180° to 185°F (80° to 85°C), the chicken is done. When the thermometer inserted into the stuffing registers 160°F (70°C), the chicken is done.

Temperature also can be measured with a handy, instant-registering thermometer which is not left in the bird during cooking but is inserted just when a reading is desired, then removed. To get a reading, remove the bird from the oven and insert the instant thermometer into the thickest section of the thigh away from bones. When it registers 180° to 185°F (80° to 85°C), the chicken is done.

Another method for determining doneness is to press the thigh and drumstick of the cooking chicken with your fingers (protect them from the heat with paper toweling). When the meat feels soft and the drumstick moves easily up and down, the chicken is done.

A third method is often used to determine doneness: piercing the skin of chicken with a fork to see when the juices run clear. This test is not always reliable, because a chicken could be done and still run juices that are slightly pink if they were located next to a bone.

Carving a Roasted Chicken

Place the cooked chicken breast-side up on a platter or carving board. For easier carving, let it stand 15 minutes after it is removed from the oven.

With a sharp carving knife, cut through the skin between the thigh and breast on one side of the chicken. Bend the thigh downward to locate the hip joint; cut through the hip joint to remove the whole leg. If desired, separate the drumstick from the thigh by cutting through the connecting joint. Repeat to remove other leg.

To remove wing, make a small cut around the shoulder joint; locate the joint. Cut through the joint and cut off the wing. Repeat to remove other wing.

Firmly insert a fork into the backbone area to hold the chicken in place. Using the tip of the knife, cut through the skin and meat slightly off to one side of the breastbone. Cut through meat until knife is pressing

CHICKEN ROASTING CHART

Type of (Whole) Bird	Ready-to-Cook Weight	Oven Temperature	Approximate Roasting Time (Stuffed or Unstuffed)
Chicken	1½ to 2¼ pounds (675 to 1015 g)	400°F (200°C)	1 to 1¼ hours
	2½ to 3 pounds (1125 to 1350 g)	375°F (190°C)	1½ to 1¾ hours
	3½ to 4 pounds (1600 to 1800 g)	375°F (190°C)	1¾ to 2¼ hours
	4½ to 5 pounds (2 kg to 2250 g)	375°F (190°C)	2½ to 2¾ hours
Rock Cornish Hen	1 to 1½ pounds (450 to 675 g)	425°F (220°C)	1 hour
Capon	5 to 7 pounds (2250 to 3150 g)	450°F (230°C) 375°F (190°C)	30 minutes 1½ to 2 hours

INTRODUCTION

against the rib bones. Cut along rib bones and through skin on underside of chicken to free breast meat. Lift breast meat away from chicken. Repeat to remove other half of breast.

Wine Selection

When choosing an appropriate wine to serve with chicken, keep in mind this general rule: delicate dishes call for lightly flavored wines, whereas hearty dishes are best with full-bodied wines.

A simple roasted chicken, for example, may be served with a light-bodied red, rosé or white wine. For chicken served with a delicate white sauce, a white or rosé wine would be a good choice. Chicken cooked in a hearty stew or a casserole could go with any wine from a delicate white to a full-bodied burgundy. If chicken is prepared with wine as an ingredient, serve the same kind of wine that was used in cooking.

White or rosé wines should be chilled before serving; red wine is best served at room temperature.

CHICKEN PREPARATION TIPS

Regardless of the cooking method used, always cook chicken completely. Do *not* partially cook it, then store it to finish cooking later.

Experiment with seasonings. When preparing a chicken for roasting or broiling, try rubbing it with one or more of the following seasonings: cayenne pepper, paprika, dried basil, marjoram, rosemary or oregano leaves. Start with about ½ teaspoon (2 mL) of seasoning for four servings.

When coating chicken with all-purpose flour for frying, dip the chicken in orange or lemon juice first. For added flavor interest, add grated orange or lemon rind to the flour. Start with about 1 teaspoon (5 mL) grated rind per ½ cup (125 mL) flour.

When pan-frying chicken, place the chicken skin-side down in the skillet so the fat will cook out of the chicken.

Always use tongs to turn chicken pieces over when frying, broiling or grilling. That will prevent the skin from being pierced and will keep the natural juices sealed inside the skin.

When broiling, it is not necessary to preheat the oven. For even browning, place the chicken 5 to 6 inches (13 to 15 cm) from the heat source.

Serve broiled chicken immediately after cooking. If it is held in a warming oven, it gets dry and tough; if placed in a covered dish, it loses its crispness.

For outdoor grilling, make a basting brush with one stalk celery with leaves, a few fresh parsley sprigs, a bay leaf and fresh mint or dill. Tie them together with string. Dip the "brush" in melted butter or basting sauce and brush over chicken.

When grilling outdoors or broiling indoors, baste chicken only during the last 30 minutes of cooking. The sauce will not penetrate during the early stages of grilling and may cause chicken to brown too quickly if added too early.

When sautéing boneless chicken breasts or other chicken pieces, use a shallow skillet if you want them to stay crisp. A deep pan creates steam.

If wine is included as an ingredient in a recipe and you do not want to use it, substitute an equal amount of chicken broth.

Reserve bones and skin when deboning chicken; refrigerate or freeze them for use in making stock, broth or soup.

For better flavor, add 2 tablespoons (30 mL) each finely chopped carrot and onion plus a sprig of fresh parsley to each 2 cups (500 mL) of canned chicken broth. Simmer about 20 minutes; strain before using.

When stuffing a chicken, allow about ¾ cup (180 mL) stuffing for each 1 pound (450 g) ready-to-cook chicken.

To bake stuffing separately, place it in a glass baking dish. Add ¼ cup (60 mL) chicken broth for each 2 cups (500 mL) stuffing. Cover and bake until done.

PREPARATION TECHNIQUES

The comprehensive section of photographed techniques that follows deserves close attention because it includes valuable information on preparing chicken for many of the recipes in this book. Among the illustrations are step-by-step directions on how to cut up chicken, how to stuff and truss chicken, and how to remove all bones from a whole chicken as well as from individual whole breasts or legs. Understanding and using the techniques illustrated here will help you save time and effort in the kitchen.

Disjointing a Whole Chicken

1. Place chicken breast-side up on cutting board. Cut between thigh and body of chicken down to hip joint. Bend leg back slightly to free hip joint from socket; cut through hip joint and remove leg. Repeat to remove other leg.

2. To separate drumstick from thigh, place leg skin-side down on cutting board. Locate joint by moving thigh back and forth with one hand while holding drumstick with other hand. Cut completely through joint.

3. Place chicken on side. Pull one wing out from body; cut through shoulder joint. Turn chicken over and repeat to remove other wing.

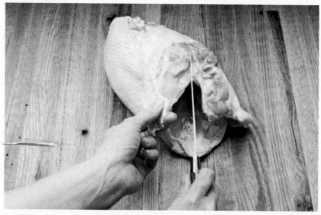

4. Working from tail toward neck, cut through skin connecting breast to backbone, cutting through small rib bones and along outside of collarbone.

5. Turn chicken over and repeat procedure on other side of chicken. Cut through any remaining connective tissue, if necessary; pull breast away from backbone.

6. Place breast skin-side up on cutting board. Split breast into halves by cutting along one side of breastbone. If desired, breastbone may be removed before splitting (see Deboning a Whole Breast, Steps 1–4).

PREPARATION TECHNIQUES

Deboning a Whole Breast

1. Place breast skin-side down on cutting board. Cut a small slit through the membrane and cartilage at the "V" of the neck end.

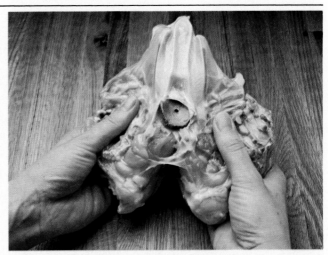

2. Grasp the breast with both hands and gently bend both sides backwards to snap the breastbone.

3. With fingers, work along both sides of the breastbone to loosen the keel bone. Pull out keel bone.

4. With tip of sharp knife, cut along both sides of the cartilage at end of breastbone. Remove cartilage.

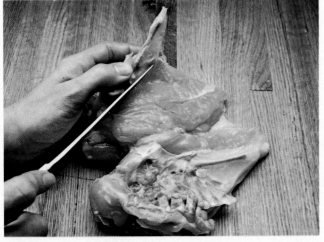

5. Slip point of knife under long rib bone on one side of breast. Cut and scrape meat from rib bones, pulling bones away from meat.

6. Cut meat away from collarbone. Remove bones. Repeat procedure to debone other side of breast.

Deboning a Whole Breast *(continued)*

7. Cut meat away from wishbone at neck end of breast. Grasp wishbone and pull it out of breast.

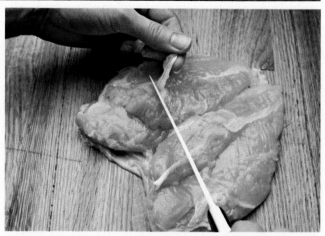

8. To remove white tendon from each side of breast, cut enough meat away from each tendon so you can grasp it (use paper toweling for firmer grasp). Pull tendon out.

Filling a Boneless Breast

9. Turn breast skin-side up. If desired, remove skin, cutting any membranes connecting it to breast. Trim breast, if necessary; cut into halves lengthwise, if desired.

1. Place breast half between two pieces of waxed paper. Pound gently to desired thickness using side of mallet or a rolling pin.

2. Fill breast as desired (filling for Chicken Kiev shown here). Fold sides and ends of breast over filling to cover completely.

3. Secure folded breast with wooden pick.

PREPARATION TECHNIQUES

Cutting Chicken into Halves and Quarters

1. Place chicken breast-side down on cutting board with neck end away from you. Working from neck to tail, cut along one side of backbone, cutting as close to bone as possible. Cut down other side of backbone; remove backbone (see Deboning a Whole Chicken, Steps 1–4).

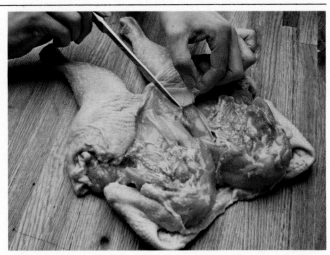

2. Remove breastbone (see Deboning a Whole Breast, Steps 1–4).

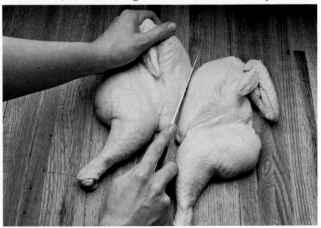

3. Turn chicken skin-side up. Cut lengthwise down center of chicken to split into halves.

4. To cut into quarters, cut through skin separating thighs from breast.

Deboning a Thigh or Whole Leg

1. To debone thigh, place thigh skin-side down on cutting board. Cut along one side of thighbone.

2. Scrape meat away from all sides of thighbone; remove bone.

Deboning a Thigh or Whole Leg (continued)

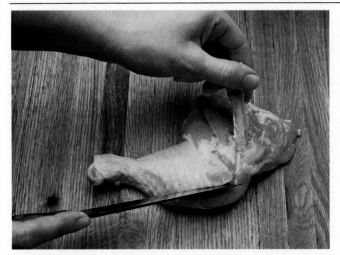

3. To debone whole leg, cut along thighbone and drumstick bone.

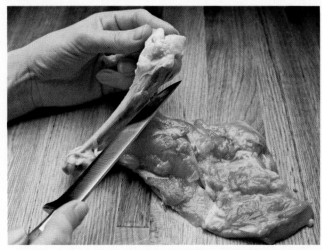

4. Scrape meat away from all sides of bones; remove bones.

Deboning a Whole Chicken

1. Place chicken breast-side down on cutting board with neck end away from you. Cut a deep slit along backbone from neck to tail.

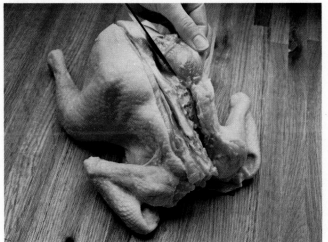

5. If desired, boneless leg can be flattened slightly; cover with waxed paper and pound gently with rolling pin or side of mallet.

2. Carefully cut meat away from backbone cutting as close to bone as possible. Gently pull all meat away from bone.

3. Cut through cartilage and small bones between breast and backbone on both sides of chicken.

Deboning a Whole Chicken *(continued)*

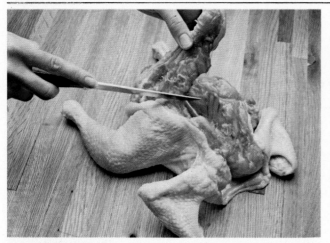

4. Cut through hip joints on both sides of chicken; lift out backbone.

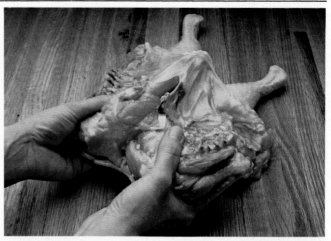

5. Remove breastbone (see Deboning a Whole Breast, Steps 1–4).

6. Remove ribs, collarbones and wishbone from breast (see Deboning a Whole Breast, Steps 5–7).

7. Cut along thighbone on one side of chicken; scrape meat away from bone. Cut through joint separating thigh from drumstick *only* if you wish to leave drumstick attached to chicken.

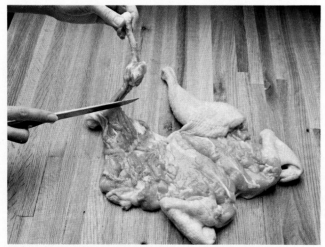

8. To debone entire leg, cut and scrape meat away from bones in thigh and drumstick. Remove and discard bones. Repeat to debone other leg.

9. Cut wings from body at shoulder joint, if desired.

Stuffing and Trussing a Chicken

1. To stuff neck cavity, place chicken breast-side down on work surface. Fill cavity loosely with stuffing.

2. Fold neck skin over stuffing to close cavity. Fasten neck skin to back with small metal skewer.

3. Turn chicken breast-side up. Fill body cavity loosely with stuffing.

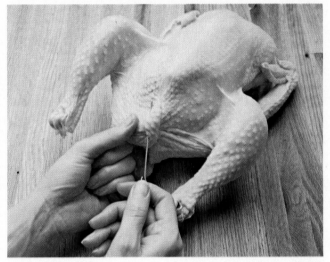

4. Overlap skin to close body cavity. Fasten skin with small metal skewer.

5. Wrap piece of string around legs and under tail. Tie string tightly so legs touch.

6. Lift ends of wings toward neck, then fold wings under chicken so the tips touch in back.

Stuffing and Trussing a Chicken *(continued)*

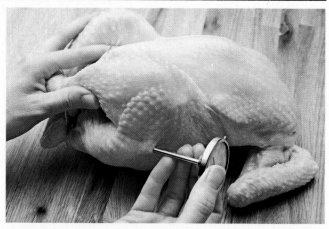

7. If using a thermometer to determine doneness, insert it into center of stuffing inside body cavity. Do not touch bone with tip of thermometer . . .

8. Or insert thermometer into one thigh, being certain tip does not touch bone.

Stuffing under the Skin

1. Place chicken breast-side up on work surface. Starting at the neck, insert fingers under the skin and carefully loosen skin from meat on one side of breast.

2. Gently loosen skin around leg; do not tear skin. Repeat procedure to loosen skin on other side of chicken.

3. Carefully push stuffing under skin of chicken to cover legs and breast.

4. Press outside of chicken with both hands to mold into smooth shape.

Appetizers

From old favorites such as Rumaki and
Chopped Chicken Livers to new discoveries such as Suez Mezze and
Chicken Wings Pakistan, this chapter offers
an assortment of tempting foods to stimulate the appetite.

Suez Mezze

Makes about 20

1 large whole chicken breast,
  deboned and skinned
1½ slices white sandwich bread
1 egg yolk
1 tablespoon (15 mL) minced
  fresh parsley
1 tablespoon (15 mL) grated
  onion
½ teaspoon (2 mL) salt
¼ teaspoon (1 mL) pepper
¼ teaspoon (1 mL) ground
  cumin
⅛ teaspoon (0.5 mL) garlic
  powder
⅛ teaspoon (0.5 mL) ground
  turmeric
⅓ cup (80 mL) all-purpose
  flour
  Vegetable oil
  Chili Peach Sauce (recipe
  follows), if desired

Appetizers are called "mezze" in the Middle East. This exotically seasoned chicken mixture is shaped into small balls before being deep fried. They can be served plain or dipped in a peach sauce.

1. Cut chicken into 1-inch (2.5 cm) pieces. Put chicken and bread through fine blade of food grinder twice, or process with metal blade in food processor until ground.

2. Place ground chicken mixture in medium bowl; mix in egg yolk, parsley, onion, salt, pepper, cumin, garlic powder and turmeric. Cover and refrigerate 30 minutes.

3. Shape mixture into balls, using 1 rounded teaspoon of the chicken mixture for each; roll each ball lightly in flour to coat.

4. Pour oil in 2-quart (2 L) saucepan to a level of 1 inch (2.5 cm). Heat oil to 350°F (180°C).

5. Fry 6 appetizers at a time in oil until golden, 3 to 4 minutes. Drain on paper toweling. Keep warm in 200°F (90°C) oven, if desired, until ready to serve.

6. Prepare Chili Peach Sauce. Serve appetizers with wooden picks and sauce for dipping.

Chili Peach Sauce

Makes 1 cup (250 mL)

½ cup (125 mL) mayonnaise
¼ cup (60 mL) chili sauce
2 tablespoons (30 mL) dry
  onion soup mix
2 tablespoons (30 mL) peach
  or apricot jam

1. Blend all ingredients in 1-quart (1 L) saucepan. Cook over low heat just until hot but not boiling.

APPETIZERS

Chicken Canapés

3   tablespoons (45 mL) cream cheese, at room temperature
1   teaspoon (5 mL) pineapple juice
¾   cup (180 mL) shredded cooked chicken
4   thin slices date-nut bread
    Thin strips (1x¼-inch or 2.5x0.5 cm) pineapple, if desired

This creamy cheese and chicken mixture is delicious spread on fresh date nut bread.

1. Blend cream cheese and pineapple juice in small bowl; mix in chicken.

2. Cut each bread slice into 4 triangles. Spread about 1 tablespoon (15 mL) of the chicken mixture evenly over each triangle. Top with 1 or 2 pineapple strips.

Variation   Prepare canapés as directed, substituting 3 tablespoons (45 mL) mayonnaise for the cream cheese and pineapple juice and mixing in 2 thinly sliced, pitted ripe olives.

Creamy Hot Chicken Spread

1   package (8 ounces or 225 g) cream cheese, at room temperature
½   cup (125 mL) sour cream
2   tablespoons (30 mL) milk
1½   cups (375 mL) finely chopped cooked chicken
3   tablespoons (45 mL) finely chopped red or green pepper
2   tablespoons (30 mL) finely chopped green onions
¼   teaspoon (1 mL) salt
¼   teaspoon (1 mL) mace
⅛   teaspoon (0.5 mL) white pepper
¼   cup (60 mL) coarsely chopped walnuts
    Thin party rye bread, pumpernickel or black bread

Nice for parties and other entertaining, this hot hors d'oeurve spread can be prepared and refrigerated hours in advance, then popped into the oven to bake just before the guests arrive.

1. Heat oven to 350°F (180°C).

2. Mix cream cheese, sour cream and milk in medium bowl. Stir in chicken, red pepper, onion, salt, mace and white pepper.

3. Spread mixture evenly into 9-inch (23 cm) pie plate; sprinkle with walnuts.*

4. Bake until hot and bubbly, about 15 minutes. Serve hot with bread.

*Note: Spread may be prepared up to this point, then covered and refrigerated for several hours. Add about 5 minutes to baking time.

Stuffed Mushroom Crowns

Makes about 50

2   cans (6 ounces or 170 g each) cooked-in-butter mushroom crowns*

1   package (3 ounces or 85 g) cream cheese, at room temperature

⅔   cup (160 mL) finely chopped cooked chicken

2   teaspoons (10 mL) lemon juice

½   teaspoon (2 mL) onion juice

⅛   teaspoon (0.5 mL) salt
    Pinch pepper
    Pinch garlic powder
    Paprika
    Small parsley sprigs, if desired

A welcome and convenient addition to any buffet table, these mushroom crowns are piled high with a creamy cheese-chicken mixture.

1. Drain mushrooms, reserve crowns. Remove and finely chop stems.

2. Combine cream cheese, mushroom stems, chicken, lemon and onion juices, salt, pepper and garlic powder in small bowl. Spoon mixture into hollow of each mushroom crown. Refrigerate at least 30 minutes.

3. Sprinkle each crown with paprika. Garnish with parsley sprig in center of each crown.

*Note: If desired, 1 pound (450 g) small fresh mushrooms can be substituted for the 2 cans cooked-in-butter mushrooms. Remove and finely chop stems. Cook mushroom crowns and chopped stems in 1 to 2 tablespoons (15 to 30 mL) butter in skillet just until brown on rounded sides, no more than 3 minutes. Proceed as directed above.

Curried Chicken Spread

Makes about 2 cups (500 mL)

1   cup (250 mL) chopped cooked chicken

2   tablespoons (30 mL) finely chopped onion

2   tablespoons (30 mL) mayonnaise

1   tablespoon (15 mL) lemon juice

½   teaspoon (2 mL) curry powder

⅛   teaspoon (0.5 mL) salt
    Dash red pepper sauce
    Pinch garlic powder

¾   cup (180 mL) finely chopped celery

⅓   cup (80 mL) finely chopped pimiento-stuffed olives

⅓   cup (80 mL) plain yogurt
    Pinch paprika
    Sliced pimiento-stuffed olives, if desired
    Assorted crackers

This richly flavored spread can be mixed quickly in a food processor or blender. Refrigerating it before serving allows the full flavor of the spices to develop.

1. Measure chicken, onion, mayonnaise, lemon juice, curry powder, salt, red pepper sauce and garlic powder into food processor or blender container. Process until thoroughly blended. (Chicken should be in small pieces.)

2. Place chicken mixture in medium mixing bowl; stir in celery, ⅓ cup (80 mL) finely chopped olives and the yogurt.

3. Transfer spread to serving bowl; sprinkle with paprika and garnish with olive slices. Cover and refrigerate 3 to 4 hours. Serve with crackers.

APPETIZERS

Mini Cream Puffs

Makes about 24

¼ cup (60 mL) water
2 tablespoons (30 mL) butter
  or margarine
¼ cup (60 mL) all-purpose
  flour
⅛ teaspoon (0.5 mL) salt
1 egg
  Cucumber Filling, Olive-
  Wine Filling or Chicken-
  Almond Filling (recipes
  follow)

These delicate puffs are delightful with any of the three distinctive fillings. They're handy appetizers for parties because both the puffs and the filling can be prepared in advance, then put together just before serving.

1. Heat oven to 400°F (200°C).

2. Place water and butter in 1-quart (1 L) saucepan. Cook over medium heat until mixture boils.

3. Add flour and salt to water mixture; stir vigorously until mixture leaves sides of pan and forms ball. Remove mixture from heat; cool slightly.

4. Add egg to flour mixture; beat vigorously until smooth.

5. Drop batter by level teaspoonsful onto large greased cookie sheet.

6. Bake until golden, 14 to 16 minutes. Remove puffs from cookie sheet. Cool on wire rack.

7. Prepare Cucumber Filling, Olive-Wine Filling or Chicken-Almond Filling.

8. Cut each puff in half horizontally. Fill bottom half of each puff with 1 heaping teaspoon of filling. Replace top half.

Cucumber Filling

Makes about 1½ cups (375 mL)

¼ cup (60 mL) plain yogurt
¼ cup (60 mL) mayonnaise
1 cup (250 mL) finely
  chopped cooked chicken
3 tablespoons (45 mL) finely
  chopped seeded
  cucumber
1 teaspoon (5 mL) minced
  fresh or dried chives
⅛ teaspoon (0.5 mL)
  seasoning salt
⅛ teaspoon (0.5 mL) dried
  dill weed

1. Blend yogurt and mayonnaise in small bowl until creamy; stir in remaining ingredients.

2. Cover and refrigerate until ready to use.

Olive-Wine Filling

Makes about 1½ cups (375 mL)

½ cup (125 mL) mayonnaise
4 teaspoons (20 mL) dry
  white wine
1 cup (250 mL) finely
  chopped cooked chicken
3 tablespoons (45 mL) finely
  chopped celery
4 pimiento-stuffed olives,
  finely chopped

1. Blend mayonnaise and wine in small bowl; stir in remaining ingredients.

2. Cover and refrigerate until ready to use.

Chicken-Almond Filling

Makes about 1¾ cups (430 mL)

¾ cup (180 mL) Whipped
  Cream Dressing (see
  Index for page number)
1 cup (250 mL) finely
  chopped cooked chicken
3 tablespoons (45 mL) finely
  chopped celery
1 teaspoon (5 mL) minced
  apple, if desired
1½ tablespoons (22 mL)
  ground blanched
  almonds

1. Prepare Whipped Cream Dressing.

2. Combine remaining ingredients in medium bowl. Fold dressing thoroughly into chicken mixture.

3. Cover and refrigerate until ready to use.

Chicken Livers à la Grecque

Makes about 30

1 pound (450 g) chicken
  livers
2 tablespoons (30 mL) fresh
  lemon juice
1 teaspoon (5 mL) dried
  oregano leaves
½ teaspoon (2 mL) salt
⅛ teaspoon (0.5 mL) pepper
Pinch garlic powder
Pinch onion powder
½ cup (125 mL) all-purpose
  flour
¼ cup (60 mL) butter or
  margarine

Fresh lemon juice and crushed oregano leaves flavor these tender, sautéed chicken livers. For entertaining, they can be served in a chafing dish so they stay hot.

1. Remove and discard fat and white tissue from chicken livers. Cut large chicken livers into halves; sprinkle with lemon juice.

2. Combine oregano, salt, pepper, garlic powder and onion powder in small bowl. Sprinkle mixture over livers.

3. Coat livers lightly with flour.

4. Melt butter in large skillet over medium heat. Add livers and cook on both sides until light brown, 3 to 4 minutes on each side. Reduce heat; cook until livers are tender, 5 to 8 minutes longer. Serve hot.

APPETIZERS

Bandito Wings

12   chicken wings
½   teaspoon (1 mL) salt
⅛   teaspoon (0.5 mL) pepper
8   tablespoons (125 mL)
      butter or margarine
2   tablespoons (30 mL)
      vegetable oil
½   cup (125 mL) taco sauce
¼   cup (60 mL) barbecue sauce
¼   cup (60 mL) French
      dressing
⅛   teaspoon (0.5 mL) red
      pepper sauce
⅛   teaspoon (0.5 mL)
      Worcestershire sauce

A snappy, Mexican-style sauce makes a tasty dip for these sautéed chicken wings.

1. Heat oven to 300°F (150°C).

2. Cut off and discard tips of each wing at first joint; cut apart the two remaining parts at the joint. Sprinkle both sides of wings with salt and pepper.

3. Heat 2 tablespoons (30 mL) butter and the oil in large skillet over medium heat.

4. Cook half the wings in the butter mixture until golden, 8 to 10 minutes on each side. Remove wings from pan and reserve. Repeat to cook remaining wings.

5. Melt remaining 6 tablespoons (90 mL) butter in 1-quart (1 L) saucepan; blend in remaining ingredients.

6. Arrange wings in shallow baking pan. Brush enough taco sauce mixture over wings to coat evenly. Bake until hot, 5 to 8 minutes.

7. Arrange wings on serving plate. Pour remaining taco sauce mixture into bowl; serve as dip for wings.

Buttery Chicken Spread

3   cups (750 mL) shredded
      cooked chicken
1   cup (250 mL) butter, at
      room temperature
¼   cup (60 mL) minced fresh
      parsley
1   tablespoon (15 mL) finely
      chopped onion
1   teaspoon (5 mL) lemon
      juice
½   teaspoon (2 mL) ground
      cinnamon
¼   teaspoon (1 mL) dried dill
      weed
      Garlic or melba toast,
      party breads or crackers

This montage of chicken, butter, parsley and aromatic seasonings makes a tempting spread for hors d'oeuvres or snacks.

1. Combine chicken, butter, parsley, onion, lemon juice, cinnamon and dill in medium bowl; mix well. Place mixture in serving dish or small crock. Cover and refrigerate 1 hour.

2. Let mixture stand at room temperature 20 minutes before serving. Serve with toast, breads or crackers.

Chinese Cocktail Wings

Makes 24

12 chicken wings
½ cup (125 mL) all-purpose
    flour
1 teaspoon (5 mL) salt
¼ teaspoon (1 mL) pepper
3 egg whites
½ cup (125 mL) fine dry
    bread crumbs
    Vegetable oil
    Grape Chutney Sauce or
    Spicy Currant Sauce
    (recipes follow)

These puffy golden wings are easy-to-eat "fun food" and will be welcome at any party. Serve them with either a zesty chutney sauce or spicy currant sauce.

1. Cut off and discard tip of each wing at first joint; cut apart the two remaining wing parts at the joint.

2. Shape each wing part so it resembles a small drumstick by scraping with sharp knife all meat from smaller to larger end of bone. On wing parts with two bones, remove and discard the smaller bone.

3. Mix flour, salt and pepper in shallow pan. Dip wings in flour mixture, turning to coat all sides evenly.

4. Beat egg whites in small bowl with fork until foamy. Dip wings in egg whites, then roll in crumbs, pressing to coat all sides evenly. Place wings on wire rack and let dry 15 minutes.

5. Meanwhile, heat oil in deep fat fryer or 2-quart (2 L) saucepan to 365°F (185°C).

6. Fry wings, a few pieces at a time, in oil until golden, 3 to 5 minutes; turn 2 or 3 times during frying to brown evenly. Drain on paper toweling. Keep warm in 200°F (90°C) oven, if desired, until ready to serve.

7. Prepare Grape Chutney Sauce or Spicy Currant Sauce. Serve chicken wings with warm sauce for dipping.

Grape Chutney Sauce

Makes about 1 cup (250 mL)

2½ tablespoons (37 mL)
    prepared mustard
½ jar (10-ounce or 285 g size)
    grape jelly
2 tablespoons (30 mL)
    chutney sauce

1. Measure ingredients into 1-quart (1 L) saucepan. Cook over low heat, stirring constantly, until jelly melts. Serve warm.

Spicy Currant Sauce

Makes about 1¼ cups (310 mL)

1 jar (10 ounces or 285 g)
    currant jelly
3 tablespoons (45 mL) Dijon-
    style mustard

1. Mix ingredients in 1-quart (1 L) saucepan. Cook over low heat, stirring constantly, until jelly melts. Serve warm.

Chicken Wings Pakistan

Makes 24

12   chicken wings
1   cup (250 mL) plain yogurt
3   tablespoons (45 mL) grated
     onion
¾   teaspoon (4 mL) salt
¾   teaspoon (4 mL) whole
     cumin seeds
½   teaspoon (2 mL) ground
     ginger
⅛   teaspoon (0.5 mL) ground
     cinnamon
⅛   teaspoon (0.5 mL) cayenne
     pepper
     Apricot Sauce (recipe
     follows), if desired

The use of cumin seed in cooking dates back to Cleopatra's days. In this recipe, it is combined with ginger and cinnamon in a tangy yogurt marinade for chicken wings.

1. Cut off and discard tip of each wing at first joint; cut apart the two remaining wing parts at the joint. Place wing pieces in shallow glass dish.

2. Blend yogurt, onion, salt, cumin seed, ginger, cinnamon and cayenne pepper in small bowl. Pour mixture evenly over wings, turning wings to coat completely. Cover and refrigerate 4 hours or overnight. Turn wings over occasionally.

3. Remove wings from yogurt mixture and place on greased broiler pan. Baste wings with yogurt mixture. Broil 6 inches (15 cm) from heat until golden, about 10 minutes. Turn wings over and baste again with remaining marinade. Broil until golden, about 5 minutes longer. Keep warm in 200°F (90°C) oven, if desired, until ready to serve.

4. Prepare Apricot Sauce. Serve wings with sauce for dipping.

Apricot Sauce

Makes about 2 cups (500 mL)

1   jar (12 ounces or 340 g)
     apricot preserves
¾   cup (180 mL) barbecue
     sauce

1. Blend ingredients in 1-quart (1 L) saucepan. Cook over low heat, stirring constantly, just until hot.

Rumaki

Makes 28

14   chicken livers
14   slices bacon, cut into
     halves
14   water chestnuts, cut into
     halves
¼   cup (60 mL) soy sauce

What better way to start a party than with the ever-popular chicken livers and water chestnuts wrapped in crispy bacon? For a zesty flavor, dip the appetizers in soy sauce before broiling.

1. Remove and discard fat and white tissue from chicken livers. Cut livers into halves.

2. Hold a chicken liver half and a water chestnut half together. Wrap a half slice bacon around them; secure with wooden pick. Repeat with remaining livers, chestnuts and bacon.

3. Carefully dip each prepared rumaki in soy sauce or brush both sides with soy sauce. Place on greased jelly roll pan or cookie sheet with sides.

4. Broil about 3 inches (8 cm) from heat until bacon is crisp, 5 to 8 minutes. Serve hot.

Mushroom Mountains

Makes about 36

1   pound (450 g) chicken
        livers
¼   cup (60 mL) butter or
        margarine
2   tablespoons (30 mL) finely
        chopped onion
2   tablespoons (30 mL) lemon
        juice
1   teaspoon (5 mL) dried
        oregano leaves
½   teaspoon (2 mL) salt
⅛   teaspoon (0.5 mL) pepper
6   ounces (170 g) cream
        cheese, at room
        temperature
1   to 1½ pounds (450 to
        675 g) small fresh
        mushrooms (about 36)
        Sliced pimiento, if desired

Who can resist fresh mushroom crowns when they are filled with chicken liver pâté? Ideal for entertaining, these delightful party appetizers can be prepared in advance and kept refrigerated until serving time.

1. Remove and discard fat and white tissue from chicken livers; cut large chicken livers into halves.

2. Melt butter in large skillet over medium heat. Add chicken livers, onion, lemon juice, oregano, salt and pepper. Cook, stirring frequently, until livers are no longer pink, about 10 minutes. Remove livers from heat and cool to lukewarm.

3. Place livers in blender or food processor container. Add cream cheese and blend until smooth, about 30 seconds. (Livers and cheese also can be placed in medium mixer bowl. Beat at high speed until smooth.)

4. Place liver mixture in bowl. Cover and refrigerate at least 3 hours.

5. Remove stems from mushrooms, reserving stems for another use. Invert caps and fill each with rounded teaspoon of liver mixture. Garnish with pimiento.

Chopped Chicken Livers

Makes about 2 cups (500 mL)

1   pound (450 g) chicken
        livers
1   cup (250 mL) finely
        chopped onion
2½   tablespoons (37 mL)
        chicken fat or butter
1   tablespoon (15 mL) hot
        water
1   teaspoon (5 mL) salt
¼   teaspoon (1 mL) pepper
3   hard-cooked eggs
1   large lettuce leaf
        Paprika
        Thin party rye bread

This classic is a Jewish tradition. The rich, chopped liver mixture tastes best when it has been refrigerated several hours to mellow the flavors.

1. Remove and discard fat and white tissue from chicken livers. Cut large chicken livers into halves. Place livers in large skillet with onion and chicken fat. Cook over medium heat until onion is golden, about 3 minutes.

2. Add hot water to skillet; cover and cook 10 minutes. Remove skillet from heat; let stand until livers cool.

3. Remove livers from skillet, reserving onion mixture. Mince livers; combine with onion mixture, salt and pepper in medium bowl.

4. Finely chop 2 of the eggs; mix into liver mixture. Cover mixture and refrigerate 4 hours or overnight.*

5. Place lettuce on serving plate; top with liver mixture. Chop white from remaining egg and sprinkle around outside edge of liver mixture. Press yolk through a sieve and sprinkle over center of liver mixture. Sprinkle with paprika. Serve with rye bread.

*Note: Mixture can be pressed into greased 2-cup (500 mL) mold before refrigerating, if desired.

APPETIZERS

Makes 24

Blue Cheese Stuffed Mushrooms

1   cup (250 mL) finely
        chopped cooked chicken
¼   cup (60 mL) finely chopped
        celery
2   tablespoons (30 mL)
        minced green onion
1   tablespoon (15 mL) minced
        fresh parsley
2   tablespoons (30 mL)
        vegetable oil
2   teaspoons (10 mL) white
        wine vinegar
1   ounce (30 g) blue cheese,
        crumbled
⅛   teaspoon (0.5 mL) dried
        oregano leaves
⅛   teaspoon (0.5 mL) garlic
        powder
    Pinch salt
    Pinch pepper
24 large fresh mushrooms, 1½
        to 2 inches (4 to 5 cm) in
        diameter
1   tablespoon (30 mL) butter
        or margarine
2   slices bacon, finely
        chopped, cooked and
        drained, if desired

For easy entertaining, these appetizing stuffed mushroom caps can be completely assembled in advance, refrigerated and then zipped under the broiler just before serving.

1. Mix chicken, celery, onion and parsley in small bowl.

2. Beat oil and vinegar in another small bowl with fork until blended; stir in cheese, oregano, garlic powder, salt and pepper. Pour cheese mixture over chicken mixture; mix well. Cover and refrigerate 30 minutes.

3. Remove stems from mushrooms and reserve for another use. Wipe mushroom caps clean with damp cloth.

4. Melt butter in large skillet over medium heat; add mushrooms, rounded side down. Cook just until mushrooms are brown on rounded sides, no more than 3 minutes. Remove from heat. Place mushrooms, rounded side down, on jelly roll pan or cookie sheet with sides.

5. Place about 2 teaspoons (10 mL) of the chicken mixture into hollow of each mushroom cap. Press mixture gently with back of spoon; sprinkle with bacon.

6. Broil about 6 inches (15 cm) from heat just until hot throughout, 2 to 3 minutes. Serve hot.

Makes about 20

Pacific Treats

2   tablespoons (30 mL)
        prepared mustard
2   tablespoons (30 mL) honey
1   large whole chicken breast,
        deboned, skinned, cut
        into 1-inch (2.5 cm)
        cubes
¾   cup (180 mL) flaked
        coconut

A tasty trio of coconut, honey and mustard are used as a coating for these cubes of chicken before they are baked. For easy eating and a festive appearance, place a wooden pick in the center of each cube before serving.

1. Heat oven to 400°F (200°C).

2. Blend mustard and honey in small bowl. Dip chicken in mustard mixture, then roll in coconut.

3. Place chicken cubes in single layer in well-greased large baking pan. Bake until chicken is golden, about 8 minutes. Turn chicken over; bake until golden, about 8 minutes longer. Serve hot.

Soups

Chicken lends itself to a variety of soups.
Choose from a delicate Consommé, hearty Brunswick Stew
or refreshing Cold Yogurt Soup.

Mulligatawny Soup

2	tablespoons (30 mL) chicken fat, butter or margarine
½	cup (125 mL) chopped onion
⅓	cup (80 mL) chopped celery
⅓	cup (80 mL) chopped carrot
1	medium apple, cored and chopped
1	quart (1 L) chicken broth
½	teaspoon (2 mL) salt
½	to 1 teaspoon (2 mL to 5 mL) curry powder
¼	teaspoon (1 mL) ground mace
¼	teaspoon (1 mL) pepper
2	cups (500 mL) finely chopped cooked chicken
1	cup (250 mL) hot cooked rice
8	tablespoons (125 mL) half and half, if desired
4	thin lemon slices, if desired Minced fresh parsley, if desired

This hearty main-dish soup derives its name from an East Indian word meaning "pepper water." For serving, the curry-flavored soup is poured over cooked rice. It needs only a green salad and crusty dinner rolls to complete the meal.

1. Melt fat in 2-quart (2 L) saucepan; add onion, celery and carrot. Cook over medium heat until onion is soft, about 4 minutes. Add apple; cook 1 minute longer.

2. Stir broth, salt, curry powder, mace and pepper into onion mixture; cook until mixture boils. Reduce heat; cover and simmer 20 minutes. Remove from heat.

3. Strain broth, reserving vegetables; return broth to saucepan. Press vegetables through sieve, or purée in blender or food processor. Stir vegetables and chicken into broth. Cook over medium heat until soup is hot.

4. Place ¼ cup (60 mL) of the cooked rice in each serving bowl. Pour hot soup over the rice. Blend 2 tablespoons (30 mL) half and half into soup in each bowl. Garnish each serving with lemon slice and minced parsley. Serve hot.

SOUPS

Old-Fashioned Noodle Soup

Makes 8 to 10 servings

1 stewing hen (about
5 pounds or 2250 g)
3 quarts (3 L) water
3 carrots, cut into 1-inch
(2.5 cm) pieces
3 stalks celery (including
leaves), cut into 1-inch
(2.5 cm) pieces
1 small onion, cut into halves
1 tablespoon (15 mL) salt
8 whole peppercorns or 1
teaspoon (5 mL) ground
pepper
1 can (16 ounces or 450 g)
tomatoes
1 cup (250 mL) thawed,
frozen peas or cut green
beans
1 cup (250 mL) thawed,
frozen whole kernel corn
2 cups (500 mL) cooked,
drained medium egg
noodles (about 4 ounces
or 115 g uncooked)

Reminiscent of grandmother's cooking, this chunky chicken noodle soup is rich with old-fashioned aroma and flavor. It can be prepared with a broiling/frying chicken, but it tastes best when made with a stewing hen.

1. Place chicken, giblets and neck in 5-quart (5 L) Dutch oven; add water. Heat to boiling over high heat; skim off foam.

2. Add carrots, celery, onion, salt and peppercorns to water; heat to boiling. Reduce heat to low; cover and simmer until thighs are tender, 2½ to 3 hours.

3. Remove chicken from broth; strain and cool broth. Skim off fat. Remove meat from chicken, discarding bones and skin. Cut enough chicken into 1-inch (2.5 cm) pieces to measure 3 cups (750 mL). Reserve remaining chicken for another use.

4. Return 2 quarts (2 L) of the broth to Dutch oven. Reserve remaining broth for another use.

5. Drain tomatoes, adding liquid to broth. Chop large tomatoes into pieces. Add tomatoes, peas and corn to broth; heat to boiling over medium heat. Cook until vegetables are done, 5 to 8 minutes.

6. Stir noodles and chicken into broth; cook until hot. Serve hot.

Herbed Chicken Soup

Makes 4 to 6 servings

2 cans (10¾ ounces or 305 g
each) condensed cream
of chicken soup
1 cup (250 mL) plain yogurt
1¼ cups (310 mL) milk or
water
½ cup (125 mL) finely
chopped cooked chicken
¾ teaspoon (4 mL) fresh or
¼ teaspoon (1 mL) dried
tarragon leaves
1 small carrot, pared and
shredded

Yogurt adds a deliciously tangy taste to this easy tarragon scented soup.

1. Place soup and yogurt in 2-quart (2 L) saucepan; stir with whisk until smooth. Blend milk into soup; add chicken and tarragon. Cook over low heat, stirring constantly, just until warm. Remove from heat. Cover and refrigerate 3 to 4 hours.

2. Pour soup into serving bowls; sprinkle with carrot.

Chicken Chowder

Makes 4 to 6 servings

¼ cup (60 mL) butter or margarine
¼ cup (60 mL) finely chopped celery
3 tablespoons (45 mL) finely chopped green onions
¼ cup (60 mL) all-purpose flour
2 cups (500 mL) milk
½ cup (125 mL) dry white wine
1 medium potato, pared, boiled and cubed
1 cup (250 mL) cubed cooked chicken
1 teaspoon (5 mL) salt
¼ teaspoon (1 mL) white pepper
Minced fresh parsley, if desired
Oyster crackers, if desired

This creamy chowder is delicious with the addition of chunks of cooked chicken. Serve it in small soup cups as a first course, or in bowls as a main course accompanied by a tossed green salad and hot buttered bread.

1. Melt butter in 2-quart (2 L) saucepan; add celery and onion. Cook over medium heat until onion is soft but not brown, about 3 minutes.

2. Blend flour into onion mixture; cook, stirring constantly, 1 minute.

3. Blend milk into flour mixture; stir in wine, potato, chicken, salt and pepper. Cook, stirring constantly, until soup boils. Reduce heat to low; simmer, stirring frequently, 5 to 7 minutes. Serve hot, garnished with parsley. Pass oyster crackers.

Golden Chicken Broth

Makes about 2½ quarts (2.5 L)

4 chicken backs
8 chicken wing tips
4 chicken necks
3 quarts (3 L) water
1 medium onion, cut into quarters
1 medium carrot, coarsely chopped
1 large stalk celery (including leaves), coarsely chopped
1 clove garlic, cut into halves
4 sprigs fresh parsley
1 teaspoon (5 mL) salt
10 whole peppercorns

Fight inflation by saving chicken backs, necks and wing tips and storing them in the freezer to make your own broth. This rich tasting broth can be used as the base for soups and sauces.

1. Place chicken parts and water in 5-quart (5 L) Dutch oven. Heat to boiling over high heat; skim off foam.

2. Add onion, carrot, celery, garlic, parsley, 1 teaspoon (5 mL) salt and the peppercorns to water. Heat to boiling. Reduce heat to low; cover and simmer about 1½ hours.

3. Strain broth through fine sieve, discarding chicken and vegetables. Cool broth; skim off fat. (Broth can be stored covered in refrigerator up to 1 week or in freezer several months.)

Italian Bean Soup

Makes 4 to 6 servings

1   package (10 ounces or
     285 g) frozen or 1 can
     (15½ ounces or 440 g)
     Italian green beans,
     drained
1   quart (1 L) chicken broth
½   cup (125 mL) tomato sauce
½   teaspoon (2 mL) salt
¼   teaspoon (1 mL) garlic salt
¼   teaspoon (1 mL) dried
     oregano leaves
⅛   teaspoon (0.5 mL) dried
     dill weed
⅛   teaspoon (0.5 mL) pepper
⅓   cup (80 mL) uncooked
     alphabet or soup
     macaroni
1   cup (250 mL) finely
     chopped cooked chicken

Nice for a light lunch or supper or as the first course of a dinner, this lightly herbed chicken soup is prepared with flat Italian green beans.

1. Place beans in 2-quart (2 L) saucepan; add broth, tomato sauce, salt, garlic salt, oregano, dill and pepper. Cook over high heat until liquid boils; stir in macaroni. Reduce heat to low; cover and simmer 10 minutes.

2. Add chicken to soup; cook 5 minutes longer. Serve hot.

Consommé

Makes 2 quarts (2 L)

2   quarts (2 L) strained
     chicken broth
2   egg whites
     Shells of 2 eggs

Consommé is the name the French give to all strained broth, stock or bouillon that has been clarified. The addition of egg white and shells helps to clarify the consommé. For added flavor, 2 tablespoons (30 mL) of Madeira wine may be stirred into each cup of hot consommé just before serving.

1. Place broth, egg whites and shells in 3-quart (3 L) saucepan. Cook over high heat until liquid boils. Reduce heat to low; simmer uncovered about 30 minutes. (To make double strength consommé, simmer until liquid is reduced to half, 30 to 40 minutes longer.)

2. Strain broth through cheesecloth. Cool; skim off fat. Serve hot or cold. (Consommé can be stored covered in refrigerator up to 1 week or in freezer several months.)

Consommé with Vermicelli or Rice Prepare consommé as directed, stirring 2 cups (500 mL) cooked drained vermicelli or 1½ cups (375 mL) cooked drained rice into hot consommé just before serving.

Chicken Noodle Soup

Makes 4 to 6 servings

1 quart (1 L) chicken broth
1 teaspoon (5 mL) instant chicken bouillon granules
¾ teaspoon (4 mL) salt
¼ teaspoon (1 mL) dried dill weed
⅛ teaspoon (0.5 mL) onion powder
⅛ teaspoon (0.5 mL) pepper
½ cup (125 mL) finely chopped cooked chicken
⅓ cup (80 mL) uncooked thin egg noodles
1 tablespoon (15 mL) dried parsley flakes

This delicate soup is delightful as the first course of a dinner.

1. Place broth, bouillon, salt, dill, onion powder and pepper in 2-quart (2 L) saucepan; cook over high heat until broth boils.

2. Stir chicken, noodles and parsley into broth; cook until broth boils. Reduce heat to low; simmer until noodles are tender, about 3 minutes. Serve hot.

Frozen Bouillon Cubes

Makes about 14 cubes

3 chicken backs
3 chicken necks
4 chicken wing tips
1½ quarts (1.5 L) water
1 large stalk celery (including leaves), cut into 2-inch (5 cm) pieces
¼ small onion
1 slice lemon
1 clove garlic
2 teaspoons (10 mL) salt
Water

This seasoned broth is boiled down to a concentrated form and then frozen in refrigerator trays. Quickly reconstituted with hot water, the frozen cubes are handy to use whenever homemade broth is desired.

1. Place chicken parts and 1½ quarts (1.5 L) water in 3-quart (3 L) saucepan. Heat to boiling over high heat; skim off foam.

2. Add celery, onion, lemon, garlic and salt to water. Heat to boiling. Reduce heat to low; simmer uncovered about 2 hours.

3. Strain broth through fine sieve, discarding chicken and vegetables. Cool broth; refrigerate.

4. Skim fat from broth. Place broth in 2-quart (2 L) saucepan. Cook over medium heat until broth boils. Continue cooking until broth is reduced to about 1 cup (250 mL). Remove from heat and cool to lukewarm.

5. Pour broth into ice cube tray. Freeze at least 4 hours. Remove cubes from tray; store cubes in plastic bags in freezer.

6. To reconstitute cubes and make 1 cup (250 mL) broth, place 1 ounce (30 g) of cubes (1 or 2 cubes) in glass measuring cup. Add enough water to make 1 cup (250 mL). Place water and cubes in small saucepan; cook over medium heat until cubes melt.

Brunswick Stew

Makes 6 to 8 servings

1   stewing chicken (about 4½ pounds or 2 kg), cut into serving pieces
2   quarts (2 L) water
1   stalk celery (including leaves), cut into 2-inch (5 cm) pieces
1   small onion, cut into quarters
1   small clove garlic, cut into halves
2   teaspoons (10 mL) salt
1   teaspoon (5 mL) whole peppercorns
1   can (16 ounces or 450 g) tomatoes, cut into 1-inch (2.5 cm) pieces
¼   cup (60 mL) tomato paste
2   medium potatoes, pared and cubed
1   onion, thinly sliced
1   teaspoon (5 mL) sugar
½   teaspoon (2 mL) ground pepper
½   teaspoon (2 mL) dried thyme leaves
⅛   teaspoon (0.5 mL) garlic powder
    Dash red pepper sauce
1   package (10 ounces or 285 g) frozen lima beans
1   package (10 ounces or 285 g) frozen whole kernel corn

This deliciously rich soup traces its roots to the plantations of the South where it was originally prepared with squirrel or rabbit.

1. Place chicken, giblets and neck in 5-quart (5 L) Dutch oven; add water. Heat to boiling over high heat; skim off foam.

2. Add celery, quartered onion, the garlic, salt and peppercorns to water; heat to boiling. Reduce heat to low; cover and simmer until thighs are tender, 2½ to 3 hours.

3. Remove chicken pieces from broth; cool slightly. Remove meat from chicken, discarding bones and skin. Cut enough chicken into 1-inch (2.5 cm) pieces to measure 3 cups (750 mL). Reserve remaining chicken for another use.

4. Strain broth through fine strainer, discarding vegetables; skim off fat. Return 1 quart (1 L) of the broth to Dutch oven. Reserve remaining broth for another use. Add tomatoes, tomato paste, potatoes, sliced onion, sugar, ground pepper, thyme, garlic powder and red pepper sauce to broth. Cook over high heat until broth boils. Reduce heat to low; cover and simmer 30 minutes.

5. Add beans and corn to stew. Cook over high heat until stew boils. Reduce heat; cover and cook 5 minutes. Add chicken cubes and cook 5 minutes longer. Serve hot.

Cold Yogurt Soup

Makes 4 servings

1   cup (250 mL) finely chopped cooked chicken
1   teaspoon (5 mL) lemon juice
¾   teaspoon (4 mL) minced fresh or ¼ teaspoon (1 mL) dried dill weed
½   teaspoon (2 mL) salt
⅛   teaspoon (0.5 mL) garlic powder
     Pinch white pepper
2   cups (500 mL) plain yogurt
1   small cucumber, seeded and diced
⅓   cup (80 mL) chopped celery
3   tablespoons (45 mL) thinly sliced green onions
     Thin radish slices or fresh dill sprig, if desired

Certain to appeal to dieters, this refreshing cold yogurt soup is enhanced with cooked chicken, diced cucumber and fresh dill.

1. Place chicken, lemon juice, dill, salt, garlic powder and pepper in small bowl; toss lightly. Cover and refrigerate 30 minutes.

2. Place yogurt in medium bowl. Stir with fork or whisk until smooth and creamy. Stir chicken mixture, cucumber, celery, and onion into yogurt.

3. Pour soup into serving bowls; garnish with radish slices.

Greek Avgolemono Soup

Makes 6 servings

1½   quarts (1.5 L) chicken broth
1   teaspoon (5 mL) salt
⅛   teaspoon (0.5 mL) pepper
½   cup (125 mL) uncooked rice
4   eggs
4   tablespoons (60 mL) fresh lemon juice
6   small fresh parsley sprigs, if desired
6   lemon wedges, if desired

This famous soup consists of golden chicken broth enriched with rice and a delicate, slightly tart blend of beaten eggs and lemon juice.

1. Place broth, salt and pepper in 3-quart (3 L) saucepan. Cook over high heat until broth boils; stir in rice. Cook until broth boils. Reduce heat to low; cover and simmer until rice is tender, 20 to 25 minutes.

2. Beat eggs with electric mixer or blender on high speed until thick and lemon colored. While continuing to beat, drizzle lemon juice, 1 tablespoon (15 mL) at a time, into eggs. Continue beating and slowly add 1 cup (250 mL) of the hot broth to the egg mixture.

3. Slowly drizzle egg mixture into remaining broth, stirring constantly. Serve immediately. (Do not cover soup; do not boil.) Garnish with parsley and serve with lemon wedges.

Salads

Cooked chicken is ideal for salad preparation.
On the following pages is a tempting array of tossed
green salads, fruit salads, vegetable plates
and spectacular molded salads, plus a variety of dressings
to go with them.

Chicken for Vegetable Salads

1   broiling/frying chicken
    (about 3 pounds or
    1350 g), cut into quarters
2   cups (500 mL) chicken
    broth
1   stalk celery (including
    leaves), cut into 2-inch
    (5 cm) pieces
½   small onion
1   small clove garlic
10 to 12 whole peppercorns
1   teaspoon (5 mL) lemon
    juice

Chicken that is to be used in vegetable salads is delicious when cooked in a seasoned broth. After cooking the chicken, strain the broth and reserve it for a soup or sauce.

1. Place all ingredients in 10-inch (25 cm) skillet.

2. Cook over high heat until boiling. Reduce heat to low. Cover and simmer until chicken is tender, about 45 minutes.

3. Remove chicken from skillet; cool. Strain broth, refrigerate and reserve for another use. Remove meat from chicken, discarding bones and skin. Cut or shred chicken as directed in selected recipe.

Chicken for Fruit Salads

1   or 2 large whole chicken
    breasts
¼   teaspoon (1 mL) salt
½   cup (125 mL) apple juice
¼   cup (60 mL) orange juice
1   teaspoon (5 mL) lemon
    juice

Chicken for fruit salads takes on a special flavor when cooked in fruit juice. Almost any canned, bottled or reconstituted frozen fruit juice can be used, as well as the juice from any fresh fruit.

1. Place chicken in medium skillet; sprinkle with salt. Pour juices into skillet.

2. Cook over high heat until boiling. Reduce heat to low. Cover and simmer until chicken is tender, about 20 minutes.

3. Remove chicken from skillet; cool. Remove meat from chicken, discarding bones and skin. Cut or shred chicken as directed in selected recipe.

Blushing Beet Ring Salad

Makes 4 to 6 main-dish servings

Chicken Macaroni Salad
   (recipe follows)
1   can (1 pound or 450 g)
       pickled beets
1   envelope (¼ ounce or 7 g)
       unflavored gelatin
¼   cup (60 mL) cold water
2¾   cups (680 mL) boiling water
2   packages (3 ounces or 85 g
       each) lemon flavor gelatin
2   tablespoons (30 mL) red
       wine vinegar
2   tablespoons (30 mL)
       prepared horseradish
1   teaspoon (5 mL) salt
2   tablespoons (30 mL) finely
       chopped onion
   Paprika, if desired

An attractive contrast of colors, the deep red gelatin ring is filled with a creamy Chicken Macaroni Salad. The salad is perfect for a party because both the ring and the chicken filling can be prepared the day before, then put together when ready to serve.

1. Prepare Chicken Macaroni Salad.

2. Drain beets, reserving liquid. Dice beets.

3. Soften unflavored gelatin in the cold water in a large bowl 1 minute. Add boiling water and lemon gelatin. Stir until gelatin is dissolved; stir in reserved beet liquid, vinegar, horseradish and salt. Refrigerate, stirring occasionally, until slightly thick, 30 to 45 minutes.

4. Fold beets and onion into gelatin mixture. Pour into oiled 6-cup (1.5 L) ring mold. Refrigerate until set, at least 4 hours.

5. Invert and unmold gelatin ring onto large serving platter; place Chicken Macaroni Salad into center. Sprinkle with paprika.

Chicken Macaroni Salad

Makes about 4 cups (1 L)

2   cups (500 mL) diced
       cooked chicken
½   cup (125 mL) small elbow
       or shell macaroni,
       cooked and drained
2   hard-cooked eggs, chopped
¾   cup (180 mL) thinly sliced
       celery
3   tablespoons (45 mL) finely
       chopped onion
2   tablespoons (30 mL) finely
       chopped green pepper
2   tablespoons (30 mL)
       shredded carrot
¾   cup (180 mL) mayonnaise
½   cup (125 mL) sour cream
2   tablespoons (30 mL) white
       wine vinegar
½   teaspoon (2 mL) Dijon-
       style mustard
1   teaspoon (5 mL) lemon
       juice
⅛   teaspoon (0.5 mL) salt
   Dash red pepper sauce

1. Place chicken, cooked macaroni, eggs, celery, onion, green pepper and carrot in large bowl; toss lightly.

2. Mix remaining ingredients in small bowl; pour over chicken mixture and toss to coat.

3. Cover and refrigerate 6 hours or overnight.

SALADS

Madrid Chicken Salad

Makes 4 main-dish servings

2 large whole chicken breasts, cooked, de-boned, skinned and cut into 1x¼-inch (2.5x0.5 cm) strips

4 oranges, peeled and sectioned

1 can (15 ounces or 425 g) artichoke hearts, drained and quartered

¼ cup (60 mL) thinly sliced green onions

16 pitted ripe olives, thinly sliced

¼ cup (60 mL) olive or vegetable oil

4 teaspoons (20 mL) wine vinegar

½ small clove garlic, pressed

1 teaspoon (5 mL) salt

⅛ (0.5 mL) teaspoon ground ginger

2 cups (500 mL) bite-size pieces endive

Julienne chicken strips, orange sections, artichoke hearts and endive mingle flavors in this Spanish-style salad.

1. Place chicken, oranges, artichokes, onions and olives in medium bowl; toss lightly.

2. Mix oil, vinegar, garlic, salt and ginger in small bowl; pour over chicken mixture and toss to coat. (At this point, salad can be refrigerated covered for several hours.)

3. Arrange endive over 4 serving plates. Place ¼ of the chicken mixture over endive on each plate.

Cantaloupe Chicken Boats

Makes 4 main-dish servings

2 cups (500 mL) diced cooked chicken

1 cup (250 mL) grapes, seeded and cut into halves

1 large orange, peeled, sectioned and cut crosswise into halves

1 apple, cored and diced

1 pear, cored and diced

3 tablespoons (45 mL) orange-flavored liqueur

2 small cantaloupes
Honey-Lemon Dressing (see Index for page number)

¼ cup (60 mL) toasted slivered almonds

Nice for a light luncheon or supper, especially during hot weather, this colorful, refreshing chicken and fruit salad is cradled inside ripe canteloupe halves.

1. Place chicken, grapes, orange, apple and pear in medium bowl. Pour liqueur over all and toss lightly until evenly coated. Cover and refrigerate 1 hour.

2. While chicken mixture is marinating, cut cantaloupes lengthwise into halves; remove seeds. Cut thin slice from bottom of each half to keep it from tipping. Cover halves with plastic wrap and refrigerate until ready to serve.

3. Prepare Honey Lemon Dressing.

4. Pour dressing over chicken mixture; toss lightly until thoroughly coated.

5. Spoon ¼ of the chicken mixture into each cantaloupe half; sprinkle with almonds.

Perfection Salad

Makes 3 to 4 main-dish servings

2 envelopes (¼ ounce or 7 g
   each) unflavored gelatin
½ cup (125 mL) cold water
1¼ cups (310 mL) boiling
   water
⅓ cup (80 mL) sugar
¼ cup (60 mL) lemon juice
3 tablespoons (45 mL) white
   wine vinegar
1¼ teaspoons (6 mL) salt
   Dash red pepper sauce
1½ cups (375 mL) chopped,
   cooked chicken
¾ cup (180 mL) shredded
   cabbage
½ cup (125 mL) chopped
   celery
⅓ cup (80 mL) shredded
   carrot
¼ cup (60 mL) sliced
   pimiento-stuffed olives
¼ cup (60 mL) thinly sliced
   radishes
2 tablespoons (30 mL) finely
   chopped onion
3 large lettuce leaves, if
   desired

This tangy molded chicken salad gets plenty of crunch and color from fresh cabbage, celery, carrot and radishes. Served with hot crusty rolls and a cold beverage, it's ideal for a refreshing summer luncheon.

1. Soften gelatin in the cold water in large bowl 1 minute; add boiling water and stir until gelatin dissolves.

2. Add sugar, lemon juice, vinegar, salt and red pepper sauce to gelatin mixture; stir until sugar dissolves. Refrigerate, stirring occasionally, until slightly thick, 30 to 45 minutes.

3. Fold chicken, cabbage, celery, carrot, olives, radishes and onion into gelatin mixture. Pour into oiled 4-cup (1 L) mold. Refrigerate until set, about 4 hours.

4. Arrange lettuce on serving plate. Invert and unmold salad onto lettuce.

Yankee Chicken Salad

Makes 2 to 3 main-dish servings

2 cups (500 mL) diced
   cooked chicken
2 tablespoons (30 mL) white
   wine vinegar
1 large potato, cooked,
   peeled and diced
½ cup (125 mL) diced celery
2 hard-cooked eggs, chopped
¼ cup (60 mL) finely chopped
   onion
1 cup (250 mL) mayonnaise
⅛ teaspoon (0.5 mL) salt
   Pinch pepper

This is a satisfying main-dish salad starring chicken, potato, celery and hard-cooked eggs.

1. Place chicken in medium bowl; sprinkle with vinegar. Let stand 15 minutes.

2. Add potato, celery, eggs and onion to chicken; toss lightly.

3. Stir mayonnaise, salt and pepper into chicken mixture. Cover and refrigerate 6 hours or overnight.

SALADS

Paella Salad

Makes 4 main-dish servings

Garlic Dressing (see Index
  for page number)
2½ cups (625 mL) water
1   cup (250 mL) uncooked
    rice
1   teaspoon (5 mL) salt
¼   to ½ teaspoon (1 to 2 mL)
    powdered saffron
2   cups (500 mL) diced
    cooked chicken
1   cup (250 mL) cooked
    deveined medium shrimp
    (about 4 ounces or 115 g)
1   cup (250 mL) diced cooked
    artichoke hearts
½   cup (125 mL) cooked peas
2   tablespoons (30 mL)
    chopped salami
2   tablespoons (30 mL) thinly
    sliced green onions
2   tablespoons (30 mL)
    chopped drained
    pimiento
1   tablespoon (15 mL) minced
    fresh parsley
    Lettuce or fresh spinach
    leaves
1   large tomato, seeded and
    cubed
4   thin lemon slices, if desired

This festive, colorful luncheon salad is adapted from the famous Spanish dish. It's made up of golden, saffron-flavored rice, cooked chicken, shrimp and artichoke hearts.

1. Prepare Garlic Dressing.

2. Place water in 1-quart (1 L) saucepan; heat to boiling over high heat. Stir rice, salt and saffron into water. Reduce heat; cover and simmer 20 minutes. Remove from heat; let stand until water is absorbed, about 5 minutes. Refrigerate until cool, about 15 minutes.

3. Place rice, chicken, shrimp, artichoke hearts, peas, salami, onions, pimiento and parsley in large bowl; toss well.

4. Pour dressing over salad; toss lightly to coat. Cover and refrigerate 1 hour.

5. Arrange lettuce on large serving platter or 4 serving plates; top with salad mixture. Garnish with tomato and lemon.

Cranberry Chicken Mold

Makes 8 to 10 servings

1   package (3 ounces or 85 g)
    raspberry flavor gelatin
1   teaspoon (5 mL) unflavored
    gelatin
1   cup (250 mL) boiling
    water
1   can (8 ounces or 225 g)
    crushed pineapple
1   cup (250 mL) canned whole
    berry cranberry sauce
    continued

This attractive gelatin salad is made up of a bright cranberry, pineapple and raspberry layer that sits atop a contrasting white chicken layer. A fluffy whipped cream dressing adds a nice finishing touch.

1. Combine raspberry gelatin and 1 teaspoon (5 mL) unflavored gelatin in medium bowl; add boiling water and stir until gelatins dissolve.

2. Drain pineapple, reserving pineapple and juice; add enough water to juice to make ½ cup (125 mL). Stir pineapple juice-water mixture into gelatin mixture. Refrigerate, stirring occasionally, until slightly thick, 30 to 45 minutes.

Cranberry Chicken Mold (continued)

2   envelopes (¼ ounce or 7 g each) unflavored gelatin
⅓   cup (80 mL) cold water
3   tablespoons (45 mL) sugar
1   tablespoon (15 mL) all-purpose flour
1   teaspoon (5 mL) salt
1   teaspoon (5 mL) dry mustard
4   egg yolks, slightly beaten
2   cups (500 mL) milk
½   cup (125 mL) cider vinegar
3   cups (750 mL) finely chopped cooked chicken
¾   cup (180 mL) finely chopped celery
3   tablespoons (45 mL) thinly sliced green onion tops
    Fluffy Mayonnaise Dressing (see Index for page number)
    Curly endive, if desired

3. Stir pineapple and cranberry sauce into gelatin mixture. Pour into oiled 2-quart (2 L) mold. Refrigerate until set, about 2 hours.

4. Soften 2 envelopes unflavored gelatin in the cold water in small bowl.

5. Combine sugar, flour, salt and mustard in medium saucepan; stir in egg yolks and milk. Slowly blend vinegar into milk mixture. Cook over medium heat, stirring constantly, until mixture is thick, about 5 minutes. Reduce heat to low; cook, stirring frequently, 10 minutes. Remove mixture from heat.

6. Stir softened gelatin into milk mixture. Refrigerate, stirring occasionally, until slightly thick, 30 to 45 minutes.

7. Fold chicken, celery and onions into milk mixture; spoon evenly into mold over set raspberry layer. Refrigerate until set, 3 to 4 hours.

8. Prepare Fluffy Mayonnaise Dressing.

9. Invert and unmold salad onto large serving platter. Garnish with endive. Serve with dressing.

Salade Port au Vin

Makes 4 main-dish servings

1   package (6 ounces or 170 g) orange flavor gelatin
2   cups (500 mL) boiling water
1   can (11 ounces or 310 g) mandarin oranges
1   can (8 ounces or 225 g) pineapple chunks
½   cup (125 mL) port wine
1½   cups (750 mL) chopped, cooked chicken
    Whipped cream, if desired
2   tablespoons (30 mL) chopped pistachio nuts, if desired

The flavor of sweet, fruity port wine predominates in this shimmering molded salad. Served with blueberry muffins, butter curls and iced tea, the salad is lovely for a luncheon on a hot summer day.

1. Combine gelatin and boiling water in medium bowl; stir until gelatin dissolves.

2. Drain oranges and pineapple, reserving a total of ½ cup (125 mL) of the liquid. Add reserved liquid and wine to gelatin mixture. Refrigerate, stirring occasionally, until slightly thick, 30 to 45 minutes.

3. Fold oranges, pineapple and chicken into gelatin mixture. Pour into oiled 6-cup (1.5 L) mold. Refrigerate until set, about 4 hours.

4. Invert and unmold salad onto serving plate. Garnish with whipped cream and sprinkle with pistachio nuts.

SALADS

Chicken Vegetable Melange

Makes 4 main-dish servings

1 package (10 ounces or 285 g) frozen chopped broccoli, cooked, drained and chilled
2 cups (500 mL) diced cooked chicken
1 can (8 ounces or 225 g) diced carrots, drained
1 can (8 ounces or 225 g) green peas, drained
1 can (8 ounces or 225 g) cut green beans, drained
½ teaspoon (2 mL) salt
⅛ teaspoon (0.5 mL) pepper
½ cup (125 mL) Russian dressing
4 large lettuce leaves
1 carton (1 pound or 450 g) large curd cream-style cottage cheese with chives

This colorful main-dish platter is coated with a zesty Russian dressing.

1. Combine broccoli, chicken, carrots, peas and beans in medium bowl; sprinkle with salt and pepper. Pour dressing over all; toss lightly to coat.

2. Arrange a lettuce leaf on each serving plate. Place ¼ of the chicken mixture on center of each lettuce leaf. Spoon about ½ cup (125 mL) of the cottage cheese around the chicken mixture on each leaf.

Florentine Salad

Makes 4 main-dish servings

½ cup (125 mL) Tarragon Dressing (see Index for page number)
1 pound (450 g) fresh spinach leaves, washed, dried and torn (about 4 cups or 1 L)
1 cup (250 mL) sliced fresh mushrooms
1 small zucchini, thinly sliced
3 green onions, thinly sliced
1 cup (250 mL) alfalfa sprouts
1 large whole chicken breast, cooked, deboned, skinned and cut into 1x¼-inch (2.5x0.5 cm) strips
2 medium tomatoes, cut into wedges

Adding cooked chicken to an enticing tossed fresh vegetable salad turns it into a delightful main dish.

1. Prepare Tarragon Dressing.

2. Place spinach, mushrooms, zucchini, onions and alfalfa sprouts in large bowl; toss lightly. Arrange chicken and tomatoes over spinach mixture. Pour dressing over all.

Paella Salad

Brunswick Stew

Bandito Wings

Cold Yogurt Soup

Blushing Beet Ring Salad

Suez Mezze

Chicken Cheese Burgers

Chicken Tabbouleh

Makes 4 main-dish servings

1   cup (250 mL) bulgur or cracked wheat
3   cups (750 mL) hot tap water
1½   to 2 pounds (675 to 900 g) chicken breasts or legs, deboned and skinned
1   teaspoon (5 mL) salt
¼   teaspoon (1 mL) pepper
2   teaspoons (10 mL) olive or vegetable oil
1   teaspoon (5 mL) butter or margarine
1   to 2 cups (250 to 500 mL) minced fresh parsley
¼   cup (60 mL) finely chopped onion
½   cup (125 mL) olive or vegetable oil
7   tablespoons (105 mL) fresh lemon juice
¼   teaspoon (1 mL) garlic powder
     Thin lemon slices, if desired

Bulgur or cracked wheat is a popular ingredient in the cuisines of several Middle Eastern countries. In this traditional salad, it is marinated with sautéed chicken cubes and fresh parsley.

1. Place bulgur in medium bowl. Pour hot water over bulgur; let stand 30 minutes.

2. Cut chicken into ½-inch (1.5 cm) cubes; sprinkle with ½ teaspoon (2 mL) of the salt and ⅛ teaspoon (0.5 mL) of the pepper.

3. Heat 2 teaspoons (10 mL) oil and the butter in large skillet over medium heat. Add chicken; cook, stirring frequently, until chicken is golden, 3 to 5 minutes. Set aside.

4. Drain bulgur and place in large bowl; add chicken, parsley, onion, ½ cup (125 mL) oil, the lemon juice, remaining ½ teaspoon (2 mL) salt, remaining ⅛ teaspoon (0.5 mL) pepper and the garlic powder. Toss well.

4. Cover and refrigerate at least 1 hour. Garnish with lemon.

Romaine Cauliflower Salad

Makes 4 main-dish servings

6   cups (1.5 L) lightly packed torn romaine leaves
1   can (16 ounces or 450 g) garbanzo beans or chick peas, drained
1   cup (250 mL) alfalfa or bean sprouts
¾   cup (180 mL) French dressing
2½   cups (625 mL) diced cooked chicken
2   cups (500 mL) fresh cauliflowerettes*
2   tablespoons (30 mL) diced drained pimiento

This main-dish salad provides an appealing contrast of colors and a harmonious blend of flavors. Accompanied by hot French bread spread with herb-flavored butter, it's ideal for an easy luncheon or supper.

1. Place romaine, garbanzos and sprouts with ½ cup (125 mL) of the French dressing in large salad bowl; toss lightly.

2. Arrange chicken and cauliflowerettes over romaine mixture; sprinkle with pimiento. Pour remaining ¼ cup (60 mL) French dressing over chicken and cauliflowerettes.

*Note: Two packages (10 ounces or 285 g each) frozen cauliflower, cooked, drained and chilled, can be substituted for the fresh cauliflowerettes. Separate cauliflower into flowerettes before adding to salad.

SALADS

Garden Salad Toss

Makes 6 main-dish servings

Sweet-Sour Dressing (see Index for page number)
2   quarts (2 L) assorted torn salad greens (romaine or Iceberg lettuce, endive, spinach or escarole)
1   small cucumber, thinly sliced
1   small green pepper, cut into 1x⅛-inch (2.5x0.5 cm) strips
½   small red onion, thinly sliced into rings
12   cherry tomatoes, cut into halves
1   cup (250 mL) fresh bean sprouts, washed and drained
3   cups (750 mL) diced cooked chicken
     Freshly ground pepper, if desired

Fresh bean sprouts are a crunchy addition to this main-dish salad that's served with a creamy sweet-sour dressing.

1. Prepare Sweet-Sour Dressing.

2. Place salad greens, cucumber, green pepper, onion, tomatoes and bean sprouts in large salad bowl; toss lightly. Pour ¾ cup (180 mL) of the dressing over salad. Gently toss salad until greens are coated.

3. Arrange chicken over top of salad. Pour remaining dressing evenly over chicken; sprinkle with ground pepper.

Tarragon Dressing

Makes 1½ cups (375 mL)

1   cup (250 mL) vegetable or olive oil
½   cup (125 mL) white wine vinegar
3   tablespoons (45 mL) fresh or 1 tablespoon (15 mL) dried tarragon leaves
1   teaspoon (5 mL) Dijon-style mustard
½   teaspoon (2 mL) salt
⅛   teaspoon (0.5 mL) pepper

With its distinctive aroma and slightly anise-like flavor, tarragon is a delightful herb to use in oil and vinegar salad dressings.

1. Mix all ingredients in tightly covered jar. (Dressing can be refrigerated up to 2 weeks.)

Fluffy Mayonnaise Dressing

Makes about 1½ cups (375 mL)

½   cup (125 mL) whipping cream, whipped
½   cup (125 mL) mayonnaise

This rich tasting yet easy-to-prepare dressing is perfect with fruit salads.

1. Fold whipped cream into mayonnaise. Serve immediately.

Whipped Cream Dressing

Makes about 3 cups (750 mL)

1 tablespoon (15 mL) butter
  or margarine
1½ tablespoons (22 mL) all-
  purpose flour
5 tablespoons (75 mL) sugar
1 egg, separated
  Pinch salt
¾ cup (180 mL) plus
  2 tablespoons (30 mL)
  pineapple juice
½ cup (125 mL) whipping
  cream

This luscious, versatile dressing goes well with most poultry or fruit salads.

1. Melt butter in 1½-quart (1.5 L) saucepan over low heat; stir in flour until smooth. Remove pan from heat.

2. Mix 4 tablespoons (60 mL) of the sugar, the egg yolk and salt in small bowl; blend into butter mixture. Stir pineapple juice into butter mixture.

3. Beat egg white in small mixer bowl at high speed until stiff but not dry; beat in remaining 1 tablespoon (15 mL) sugar.

4. Stir egg white mixture into butter mixture; cook over low heat, stirring occasionally, 5 minutes longer.

5. Pour mixture into large bowl; cover and refrigerate until cold, about 30 minutes.

6. Beat cream in small mixer bowl at high speed until stiff but not dry. Fold cream into egg mixture. (Dressing can be refrigerated covered up to 3 days.)

Honey-Lemon Dressing

Makes about ½ cup (125 mL)

⅓ cup (80 mL) honey
¼ cup (60 mL) lemon juice
1 tablespoon (15 mL)
  powdered sugar
⅛ teaspoon (0.5 mL) ground
  nutmeg
  Pinch salt

Try this easy dressing over cold cooked chicken or with poultry and/or fruit salads.

1. Mix all ingredients in a small bowl. (Dressing can be refrigerated covered up to 2 weeks.)

Celery Seed Dressing

Makes about 1 cup (250 mL)

1 cup (250 mL) mayonnaise
2 tablespoons (30 mL) white
  wine vinegar
1 tablespoon (15 mL) sugar
½ teaspoon (2 mL) salt
½ teaspoon (2 mL) dry
  mustard
½ teaspoon (2 mL) celery
  seeds
⅛ teaspoon (0.5 mL) pepper

Celery seeds add delightful seasoning to salad dressings. They enhance the flavor of an oil and vinegar-style or a mayonnaise dressing such as this.

1. Mix all ingredients in tightly covered jar. (Dressing can be refrigerated up to 2 weeks.)

SALADS

Cucumber Dressing

Makes 1½ cups (375 mL)

1   medium cucumber, peeled,
        seeded and chopped
1   cup (250 mL) plain yogurt
1½   teaspoons (7 mL) minced
        fresh or ½ teaspoon
        (2 mL) dried dill weed
⅛   teaspoon (0.5 mL) salt
⅛   teaspoon (0.5 mL) garlic
        powder
        Pinch white pepper

For the weight conscious, this cool-as-a-cucumber dressing is perfectly suited for any salad combination of torn fresh greens and chilled poultry strips.

1. Squeeze cucumber to remove excess moisture.

2. Mix cucumber with remaining ingredients in small bowl. Cover and refrigerate at least 1 hour. (Dressing can be refrigerated covered up to 5 days.)

Sweet-Sour Dressing

Makes about 1 cup (250 mL)

½   cup (125 mL) mayonnaise
½   cup (125 mL) plain yogurt
2   tablespoons (30 mL) vinegar
1½   tablespoons (22 mL) sugar
¼   teaspoon (1 mL) dry
        mustard
¼   teaspoon (1 mL) salt

This creamy, slightly sweet, slightly tangy dressing is perfect with leafy green salads.

1. Measure all ingredients into small bowl. Beat with whisk until blended. Cover and refrigerate until serving. (Dressing can be refrigerated covered up to 5 days.)

Creamy Cranberry Dressing

Makes 1 cup (250 mL)

¼   cup (60 mL) jellied
        cranberry sauce
½   cup (125 mL) plain yogurt
¼   cup (60 mL) mayonnaise

This colorful dressing is a fine compliment to your favorite poultry and fruit salads.

1. Beat cranberry sauce in small bowl with a whisk until almost smooth. Blend in yogurt and mayonnaise. (Dressing can be refrigerated covered up to 5 days.)

Garlic Dressing

Makes 1 cup (250 mL)

¾   cup (180 mL) olive or
        vegetable oil
¼   cup (60 mL) white wine
        vinegar
1   teaspoon (5 mL) salt
½   teaspoon (2 mL) pepper
1   clove garlic, pressed

This simple oil and vinegar dressing can be served with any chicken and vegetable salad.

1. Mix all ingredients in tightly covered jar. (Dressing can be refrigerated up to 2 weeks.)

Sandwiches

Submarines, Monte Cristos, Grilled Reubens,
Heroes, Burgers and Dagwood-Style sandwiches—this chapter
has the recipes for all of these classics,
and more.

Stroganoff Sandwich

Makes 2 sandwiches

Chicken replaces beef in this version of the popular Russian dish that is served over toasted French rolls.

2   tablespoons (30 mL) butter or margarine
1   large whole chicken breast, deboned, skinned and cut into ¼-inch (0.5 cm) wide strips
½   teaspoon (2 mL) salt
⅛   teaspoon (0.5 mL) garlic powder
⅛   teaspoon (0.5 mL) pepper
1   cup (250 mL) thinly sliced mushrooms
½   cup (125 mL) thinly sliced onion
1   teaspoon (5 mL) all-purpose flour
¼   teaspoon (1 mL) Worcestershire sauce
⅛   teaspoon (0.5 mL) dry mustard
1   tablespoon (15 mL) dry sherry
½   cup (125 mL) sour cream
2   French rolls (each about 6½ inches or 16.5 cm long), cut horizontally into halves and toasted
½   cup (125 mL) shredded lettuce
1   small tomato, cut into thin slices

1. Melt butter in large skillet over medium heat; add chicken, salt, garlic powder and pepper. Cook, stirring occasionally, 5 minutes.

2. Add mushrooms and onion to chicken mixture; cook until onion is golden, about 5 minutes.

3. Stir flour, Worcestershire sauce and mustard into chicken mixture; cook 1 minute longer.

4. Add sherry to chicken mixture; cook until sherry evaporates, about 1 minute longer.

5. Place sour cream in small bowl; stir in about 2 tablespoons (30 mL) of the hot chicken mixture. Slowly stir sour cream mixture into chicken mixture in skillet. Cook over low heat just until hot; do not boil.

6. Spoon half of the chicken mixture over bottom half of each roll; top with lettuce, tomato and top half of roll. Serve hot.

SANDWICHES

Makes 4 servings

Chicken Sandwich Supreme

Yogurt Thousand Island
Dressing (recipe follows)
4 slices rye bread
½ small head Iceberg lettuce,
  cut into 4 slices about
  ½-inch (1.5 cm) thick
  each
4 slices (about 1 ounce or
  30 g each) Swiss cheese
1 large whole chicken breast,
  cooked, deboned,
  skinned, and cut into
  ⅛-inch (0.5 cm) thick
  slices
4 slices bacon, cut into
  halves, crisply cooked
  and drained
4 slices tomato

These sensational, open-faced sandwiches feature chicken, Swiss cheese and lettuce on rye bread. They're topped with a zesty yogurt dressing.

1. Prepare Yogurt Thousand Island Dressing.

2. Place each slice bread on a serving plate; top each with 1 slice lettuce and 1 slice cheese. Arrange chicken slices evenly over cheese.

3. Pour about ¼ cup (60 mL) of the dressing over each sandwich. Arrange bacon halves criss-cross on top of each sandwich; top with tomato. Serve.

Makes about 1 cup (250 mL)

Yogurt Thousand Island Dressing

¾ cup (180 mL) plain yogurt
1½ tablespoons (22 mL)
  mayonnaise
1½ tablespoons (22 mL) chili
  sauce
1½ tablespoons (22 mL) pickle
  relish
1 tablespoon (15 mL) finely
  chopped pimiento
1 hard-cooked egg, chopped
½ teaspoon (2 mL) sugar
½ teaspoon (2 mL) instant
  minced onion

1. Blend all ingredients in small bowl.

Chickenburgers

1   teaspoon (10 mL) Seasoned Salt (see Index for page number)
2   cups (500 mL) finely chopped cooked chicken
⅓   cup (80 mL) mayonnaise
1   teaspoon (5 mL) minced celery leaves
1   cup (250 mL) corn flake crumbs
2   tablespoons (30 mL) butter or margarine
1   tablespoon (15 mL) vegetable oil
4   hamburger buns, cut horizontally into halves
4   thin slices tomato
4   tablespoons (60 mL) shredded lettuce

For a change of pace from traditional hamburgers, try these tasty chickenburgers.

1. Prepare Seasoned Salt.

2. Mix chicken, mayonnaise and celery leaves in medium bowl. Shape mixture into 4 round patties; dip on both sides in corn flake crumbs, pressing to coat well.

3. Heat butter and oil in large skillet over medium heat; add patties. Cook until patties are golden, 2 to 3 minutes on each side.

4. Place 1 patty on bottom half of each hamburger bun; top each with 1 tomato slice and 1 tablespoon (15 mL) of the lettuce. Serve hot.

Towering Chicken Sandwich

⅓   cup (80 mL) crumbled cooked bacon (about 5 slices)
3   tablespoons (45 mL) orange marmalade
12 slices square pumpernickel or whole wheat bread
2   whole chicken breasts, cooked, skinned, deboned and thinly sliced
4   lettuce leaves
⅓   cup (80 mL) mayonnaise
1   tablespoon (15 mL) prepared mustard
1   teaspoon (5 mL) prepared horseradish
4   large thin slices tomato
4   thin slices Bermuda onion
4   slices (about 1 ounce or 30 g each) Swiss cheese

Reminiscent of a Dagwood sandwich, this triple-decker club sandwich has all the ingredients needed to make it a family favorite.

1. Mix bacon and marmalade in small bowl; spread about 2 tablespoons (30 mL) of the marmalade mixture over each of 4 slices bread. Top each slice with ¼ of the chicken slices and a lettuce leaf.

2. Blend mayonnaise, mustard and horseradish in small bowl; spread half of the mixture evenly over 4 slices bread. Place slices, mayonnaise-side down, on top of lettuce.

3. Place one slice each tomato, onion and cheese on top of bread in each sandwich.

4. Spread remaining 4 slices bread with remaining mayonnaise mixture. Place slices, mayonnaise-side down, on each sandwich. Secure with wooden picks. Cut each sandwich into quarters. Serve.

SANDWICHES

Grilled Chicken Reuben

Makes 2 sandwiches

¼ cup (60 mL) mayonnaise
1 teaspoon (5 mL) chili sauce
2 pimiento-stuffed olives, chopped
4 large slices pumpernickel bread
2 slices (each 7x3½ inches or 18x9 cm) Swiss cheese (about 1½ to 2 ounces or 45 to 60 g each)
1 whole chicken breast, cooked, deboned, skinned and thinly sliced
6 tablespoons (90 mL) well-drained sauerkraut
4 thin slices corned beef
4 teaspoons (20 mL) butter or margarine, at room temperature

Thin slices of cooked chicken are tucked between the corned beef and sauerkraut in these scrumptious grilled sandwiches.

1. Mix mayonnaise, chili sauce and olives in small bowl. Spread about 1 tablespoon (15 mL) of the mixture over one side of each slice bread.

2. Top each of 2 slices bread with 1 slice cheese, half of the chicken slices, 3 tablespoons (45 mL) of the sauerkraut and 2 slices corned beef; cover with remaining bread slices, spread-side down. Spread 1 teaspoon (5 mL) butter over each side of each finished sandwich.

3. Place sandwiches in large skillet or on griddle. Cover and cook over medium heat until bread is toasted, 2 to 4 minutes. Turn sandwiches over. Cover and cook until bread is toasted and cheese melts, 2 to 4 minutes longer. Serve hot.

Sherried Liver Sandwich

Makes 4 servings

1 pound (450 g) chicken livers
½ teaspoon (2 mL) salt
Pinch pepper
¼ cup (60 mL) all-purpose flour
½ cup (125 mL) butter or margarine
2 cups (500 mL) diagonally sliced celery
¼ cup (60 mL) chopped onion
2 tablespoons (30 mL) minced celery leaves
1 cup (250 mL) thinly sliced fresh mushrooms
¼ cup (60 mL) dry sherry
4 slices sandwich bread
1 tomato, peeled, seeded and cubed, if desired
Parsley sprigs, if desired

For those who are fond of chicken livers, this celery-flavored combination served over toast points makes a welcome Sunday brunch offering.

1. Remove and discard fat and white tissue from livers. Cut large livers into halves; sprinkle with salt and pepper. Coat livers lightly with flour.

2. Melt ¼ cup (60 mL) of the butter in large skillet over medium heat; add celery, onion and celery leaves. Cook, stirring occasionally, until celery is slightly soft, about 5 minutes. Remove celery mixture from skillet; reserve.

3. Melt remaining ¼ cup (60 mL) butter in the skillet; add livers and mushrooms. Cook, stirring occasionally, until livers are no longer pink, about 10 minutes. Stir celery mixture and sherry into liver mixture. Cook until hot. Keep warm.

4. Remove and discard crusts from bread. Toast until golden. Cut each slice in half diagonally; arrange 2 halves on each of 4 serving plates.

5. Spoon liver mixture over toast; garnish with tomato and parsley. Serve hot.

Submarine Sandwich

Makes 4 sandwiches

This version of the popular hero sandwich is sure to be a winner. It features plenty of layers of tempting sandwich fixings stacked high inside French rolls.

4   tablespoons (60 mL) Sassy Sandwich Spread (recipe follows)

4   French rolls (each about 6½ inches or 16.5 cm long), cut horizontally into halves

1   cup (250 mL) shredded lettuce

4   slices (each about 7x3½ inches or 18x9 cm) brick cheese (about 1½ to 2 ounces or 45 to 60 g each)

4   slices (each about 7x3½ inches or 18x9 cm) boiled ham (about 1½ to 2 ounces or 45 to 60 g each)

8   thin slices salami

2   whole chicken breasts, cooked, deboned, skinned and cut into thin slices

8   thin slices tomato

8   thin rings green pepper

1   small red onion, thinly sliced

1. Prepare Sassy Sandwich Spread. Spread ½ tablespoon (7 mL) of the spread over cut surface of each roll half.

2. Arrange ¼ cup (60 mL) of the lettuce over bottom half of each roll; top each with 1 slice cheese, 1 slice ham and 2 slices salami. Arrange ¼ of the chicken slices over salami on each roll; top each with 2 tomato slices, 2 rings green pepper and 2 or 3 slices onion. Cover each sandwich with top half of roll. Serve.

Sassy Sandwich Spread

Makes 1 cup (250 mL)

2   teaspoons (10 mL) Seasoned Salt (see Index for page number)

1   cup (250 mL) mayonnaise

2   tablespoons (30 mL) cider vinegar or Italian salad dressing

2   teaspoons (10 mL) prepared mustard

½   teaspoon (2 mL) onion powder

Pinch garlic powder

1. Prepare Seasoned Salt.

2. Mix Seasoned Salt and all remaining ingredients in small bowl; cover and refrigerate. (Spread can be refrigerated covered up to 2 weeks.)

SANDWICHES

Broiled Chicken Treats

Makes 2 to 4 servings

½ package (3 ounce or 85 g size) cream cheese, at room temperature
2 tablespoons (30 mL) chili sauce
¼ teaspoon (1 mL) instant minced onion
¼ teaspoon (1 mL) prepared horseradish
¼ teaspoon (1 mL) Worcestershire sauce
½ cup (125 mL) finely chopped cooked chicken
1 tablespoon (15 mL) sweet pickle relish
4 slices sandwich bread, crusts removed
1 tablespoon (15 mL) butter or margarine, at room temperature
1 to 2 tablespoons (15 to 30 mL) grated Parmesan cheese
4 pitted ripe olives, cut into thin slices
4 fresh parsley sprigs, if desired

These snappy little sandwiches are perfect for light lunches or afternoon snacks.

1. Blend cream cheese, chili sauce, onion, horseradish and Worcestershire sauce in small bowl until smooth; mix in chicken and relish.

2. Spread bread slices with butter. Spread each slice evenly with about 2 tablespoons (30 mL) of the chicken mixture; sprinkle with Parmesan cheese.

3. Broil slices 6 inches (15 cm) from heat until cheese melts, about 2 minutes. Serve hot, garnished with olives and parsley.

Monte Cristo Sandwich

Makes 4 sandwiches

8 slices white sandwich bread
4 slices (each 3½ inches or 9 cm square) Swiss cheese (about 1 ounce or 30 g each)
4 slices (each 3½ inches or 9 cm square) cooked ham (about 1 ounce or 30 g each)
1 large whole chicken breast, cooked, deboned, skinned and thinly sliced
¼ teaspoon (1 mL) ground nutmeg *continued*

These hearty ham, chicken and cheese sandwiches are battered-dipped and then grilled until golden. They're delicious served hot accompanied by strawberry-flavored yogurt.

1. Cover each of 4 slices bread with 1 slice cheese and 1 slice ham. Arrange chicken slices evenly over ham; sprinkle with nutmeg and salt.

2. Cover each sandwich with a remaining bread slice; cut each sandwich in half diagonally.

3. Brush griddle with butter; heat griddle to 350°F (180°C).

4. Beat eggs and milk in shallow pan. Dip sandwich halves into egg mixture, coating both sides. Cook sandwiches on griddle until golden and hot throughout, 3 to 5 minutes on each side.

Monte Cristo Sandwich *(continued)*

Pinch salt
1 tablespoon (15 mL) butter
 or margarine, at room
 temperature
2 eggs
½ cup (125 mL) milk
2 tablespoons (30 mL)
 strawberry preserves, if
 desired
1 cup (250 mL) plain yogurt,
 if desired

5. Stir strawberry preserves into yogurt. Serve sandwiches hot with yogurt mixture for dipping.

Chicken Cheese Burgers

Makes 4 servings

3 cups (750 mL) ground raw
 chicken
2 eggs, slightly beaten
1 small onion, finely chopped
2 tablespoons (30 mL) fine
 dry bread crumbs
2 tablespoons (30 mL)
 minced fresh parsley
1 tablespoon (15 mL) grated
 Parmesan cheese
1 teaspoon (5 mL) salt
¼ teaspoon (1 mL) baking
 soda
¼ teaspoon (1 mL) white
 pepper
¼ teaspoon (1 mL) dried
 oregano leaves
2 tablespoons (30 mL) butter
 or margarine
2 tablespoons (30 mL)
 vegetable oil
4 slices American or Cheddar
 cheese (each about
 1 ounce or 30 g)
4 large hamburger buns, cut
 horizontally into halves
4 tablespoons (60 mL)
 mayonnaise
4 leaves lettuce
4 to 8 slices tomato

Chicken takes on a new look and a wonderful taste when it's made into a burger and served on buns with cheese, lettuce and tomato.

1. Combine chicken, eggs, onion, bread crumbs, parsley, Parmesan cheese, salt, baking soda, pepper, and oregano in large bowl; mix well. Shape chicken mixture into 4 round patties.

2. Heat butter and oil in large skillet over medium-low heat until butter melts; add patties. Cook until patties are golden, 4 to 5 minutes on each side.

3. Place 1 slice cheese on top of each patty. Cover skillet; cook until cheese melts, about 1 minute.

4. Spread each bun with 1 tablespoon (15 mL) of the mayonnaise. Arrange a lettuce leaf over bottom half of each bun; top with a patty, 1 or 2 tomato slices and top half of bun. Serve hot.

SANDWICHES

Chicken Curry Snacks

Makes 4 servings

3   tablespoons (45 mL) butter or margarine
1   cup (250 mL) chopped cooked chicken
½   cup (125 mL) chopped cooked ham
2   green onions, thinly sliced
2   tablespoons (30 mL) all-purpose flour
1   cup (250 mL) half and half
¼   teaspoon (1 mL) curry powder
⅛   teaspoon (0.5 mL) salt
4   slices white bread, toasted
4   slices (each 3½ inches or 9 cm square) American, Cheddar or brick cheese (about 1 ounce or 30 g each)
   Curly endive, if desired
1   small tomato, cut into 4 wedges, if desired
4   pimiento-stuffed olives, if desired

Curry powder lightly flavors these toasty sandwiches that are served piping hot topped with melted cheese.

1. Melt butter in medium saucepan over medium heat; add chicken, ham and onion. Cook until onion is soft, about 3 minutes.

2. Stir flour into chicken mixture; cook 1 minute longer.

3. Blend half and half into chicken mixture; add curry powder and salt. Cook, stirring constantly, until thick, 3 to 5 minutes. Remove from heat.

4. Spread ¼ of the chicken mixture evenly over each toast slice; top with cheese.

5. Broil about 5 inches (13 cm) from heat until cheese melts, 2 to 3 minutes.

6. Garnish sandwiches with endive, tomato wedges and olives. Serve hot.

Danish Smørrebrød

Makes 2 sandwiches

2   slices rye, pumpernickel or whole grain bread
4   teaspoons (20 mL) mayonnaise
2   lettuce leaves
1   large whole chicken breast, cooked, deboned, skinned and cut into thin slices
4   tablespoons (60 mL) finely chopped apple
2   tablespoons (30 mL) finely chopped carrot
1   tablespoon (15 mL) mayonnaise
1   small thin orange slice, cut into halves

Cooked chicken is a perfect addition to these famous Danish open-faced sandwiches.

1. Spread each slice bread with 2 teaspoons (10 mL) of the mayonnaise; cover each with a lettuce leaf.

2. Top each lettuce leaf with half of the chicken.

3. Mix apple, carrot and 1 tablespoon (15 mL) mayonnaise in small bowl; spoon half of the mixture over chicken on each sandwich.

4. Twist each half orange slice and place in center of apple mixture. Serve.

Grecian Kabobs in Pita Bread

Makes 4 servings

¼ cup (60 mL) olive or
  vegetable oil
¼ cup (60 mL) lemon juice
½ teaspoon (2 mL) salt
½ teaspoon (2 mL) dried
  oregano leaves
¼ teaspoon (1 mL) garlic
  powder
⅛ teaspoon (0.5 mL) pepper
1 large, whole chicken
  breast, deboned, skinned
  and cut into 1-inch
  (2.5 cm) cubes
2 large pita breads
1 small onion, thinly sliced
1 tomato, thinly sliced
½ cup (125 mL) plain yogurt
  Parsley, if desired

These skewered chicken cubes are marinated in an aromatic herb sauce before grilling. They're delicious served inside pita bread and topped with onion, tomato and yogurt. They also can be served over hot, buttered white or brown rice.

1. Mix oil, lemon juice, salt, oregano, garlic powder and pepper in medium glass bowl.

2. Add chicken to oil mixture; toss to coat completely. Cover and refrigerate at least 3 hours or overnight.

3. Remove chicken from marinade, reserving marinade. Thread chicken onto 4 small metal skewers. Reserve.

4. Place kabobs on greased broiler pan. Broil about 5 inches (13 cm) from heat until chicken is golden, 8 to 10 minutes; brushing frequently with marinade. Turn kabobs over and brush with marinade. Broil until chicken is done, 5 to 7 minutes longer.

5. Cut each pita bread in half; gently pull each half open to form a pocket. Remove chicken from 1 kabob and place inside each pocket; top with onion, tomato and yogurt. Garnish with parsley. Serve hot.

Chicken Hero

Makes 4 sandwiches

1 cup (250 mL) shredded
  cooked chicken
¼ cup (60 mL) finely chopped
  celery
8 pimiento-stuffed olives,
  finely chopped
1 hard-cooked egg, chopped
1 tablespoon (15 mL) pickle
  relish
1 tablespoon (15 mL) finely
  chopped onion
½ teaspoon (2 mL) salt
6 tablespoons (90 mL)
  mayonnaise
4 hot dog buns, cut
  horizontally into halves
4 small lettuce leaves
4 slices American cheese
  (about 1 ounce or
  30 g each)

This variation of the popular hero sandwich consists of chicken salad, lettuce and American cheese layered on hot dog buns.

1. Mix chicken, celery, olives, egg, relish, onion and salt in medium bowl; add mayonnaise and toss lightly until all ingredients are coated.

2. Cover bottom half of each bun with a lettuce leaf.

3. Cut each cheese slice into ½-inch (1.5 cm) wide strips; arrange strips over lettuce.

4. Spread ¼ of the chicken mixture over cheese on each bun; cover with bun tops.

SANDWICHES

Sombrero Sandwich

Makes 4 servings

2   teaspoons (10 mL)
     vegetable oil
4   small corn tortillas (each
     6 inches or 15 cm in
     diameter)
1   can (15 ounces or 425 g)
     Mexican-style chili beans
     or red kidney beans
3   tablespoons (45 mL)
     vegetable oil
¾   teaspoon (4 mL) chili
     powder
1   ripe avocado
1   tablespoon (15 mL) lemon
     juice
1   green chile, finely chopped
1   tomato, peeled, seeded and
     chopped
1   tablespoon (15 mL) finely
     chopped onion
¼   teaspoon (1 mL) salt
     Dash red pepper sauce
2   teaspoons (10 mL) butter
     or margarine
¾   cup (180 mL) chopped
     cooked chicken
4   tablespoons (60 mL) sour
     cream

This is a delicious combination of refried beans, sautéed chicken and guacamole served atop crisp tortillas. A dollop of sour cream completes this colorful sandwich.

1. Heat ½ teaspoon (2 mL) of the oil in medium skillet over medium heat. Cook a tortilla in the oil until crisp, about 1 minute on each side; drain on paper toweling. Repeat to cook remaining tortillas, using ½ teaspoon (2 mL) oil for each. Place tortillas on cookie sheet and keep warm in 200°F (90°C) oven.

2. Drain beans, reserving ¼ cup (60 mL) of the liquid. Mash beans in large skillet with fork; add 3 tablespoons (45 mL) oil, the chili powder and reserved ¼ cup (60 mL) bean liquid. Cover and cook over medium heat, stirring occasionally, until all liquid evaporates, about 10 minutes. Keep warm.

3. Remove and discard peel and seed from avocado. Mash avocado with lemon juice in small bowl; mix in green chile, tomato, onion, salt and red pepper sauce.

4. Melt butter in small skillet over medium heat. Add chicken to skillet; cook until hot.

5. Place a tortilla on each of 4 serving plates. Spread ¼ of the bean mixture over each tortilla; top each with ¼ of the chicken, ¼ of the avocado mixture and 1 tablespoon (15 mL) of the sour cream. Serve.

Luncheon

On the next few pages, you'll find recipes that make
any luncheon special. A quick-to-fix Chicken Liver Omelet,
a delectable Chicken Souffle and
posh Shrimp and Chicken in Brioches are just a sampling
of the delightful offerings.

Chicken Souffle

Makes 5 to 6 servings

4   to 5 tablespoons (60 to 75 mL) butter or margarine, at room temperature

2   to 3 tablespoons (30 to 45 mL) grated Parmesan cheese

1½   cups (375 mL) finely chopped cooked chicken

1   teaspoon (5 mL) finely chopped onion

¼   cup (60 mL) all-purpose flour

2   teaspoons (10 mL) minced fresh parsley

1   cup (250 mL) half and half

½   teaspoon (2 mL) salt

¼   teaspoon (1 mL) ground nutmeg

⅛   teaspoon (0.5 mL) white pepper

6   Large egg yolks

½   cup (125 mL) shredded Swiss cheese (2 ounces or 60 g)

7   Large egg whites, at room temperature

½   teaspoon (2 mL) cream of tartar

Louisiana Creole Sauce, if desired (see Index for page number)

This spectacular souffle is easily within reach of any cook. The secret to its success lies in the egg whites—they must be beaten long enough so they no longer slide when the bowl is tilted. Once the souffle comes out of the oven, it must be served immediately.

1. Coat inside of 2-quart (2 L) souffle dish evenly with 1 to 2 tablespoons (15 to 30 mL) of the butter; sprinkle with Parmesan cheese.

2. Melt remaining 3 tablespoons (45 mL) butter in 2-quart (2 L) saucepan over medium heat; add chicken and onion. Cook until chicken is golden, about 5 minutes; stir in flour and parsley. Cook over low heat, stirring constantly, 1 minute.

3. Blend half and half gradually into flour mixture; add salt, nutmeg and pepper. Cook over medium heat, stirring constantly, until thick, about 5 minutes. Remove from heat.

4. Beat egg yolks lightly in small bowl with whisk. Stir ¼ cup (60 mL) of the chicken mixture into beaten yolks. Stir yolk mixture into chicken mixture; mix in Swiss cheese.*

5. Heat oven to 350°F (180°C).

6. Beat egg whites and cream of tartar in large mixer bowl at high speed just until whites no longer slip when bowl is tilted. (Do not overbeat.) Fold whites gently but thoroughly into chicken mixture.

7. Pour mixture into souffle dish. Bake until golden and souffle shakes slightly when oven rack is moved back and forth, 40 to 45 minutes.

8. While souffle is baking, prepare Louisiana Creole Sauce. Serve souffle immediately after it is removed from oven. Pass sauce to spoon over souffle.

*Note: Souffle can be prepared up to this point, covered and refrigerated several hours. To complete souffle, cook chicken mixture in saucepan over low heat, stirring frequently, until hot. Remove from heat; proceed as directed.

Chicken Vesuvio Crepes

Makes 4 to 6 servings

These tempting crepes are filled with a medley of vegetables and chicken and topped with a light tomato sauce.

Tomato Wine Salsa (recipe follows)
Crepes (recipe follows)
1 cup (250 mL) cubed uncooked pared potatoes
1 tablespoon (15 mL) olive oil
2 cups (500 mL) chopped cooked chicken
1 cup (250 mL) sliced fresh mushrooms
1 medium green pepper, cut into 1x⅛-inch (2.5x0.5 cm) strips
⅓ cup (80 mL) thinly sliced onion
½ teaspoon (2 mL) salt
¼ teaspoon (1 mL) ground pepper
Pinch garlic powder
2 tablespoons (30 mL) dry red wine
2 ounces (60 g) Monterey Jack cheese, cut into 24 strips (about 2½x¼-inch or 6.5x0.5 cm)

1. Prepare Tomato Wine Salsa. Spread ¼ cup (60 mL) of the Salsa evenly over bottom of each of two 11x7x1½-inch (28x18x4 cm) baking dishes; reserve.

2. Prepare Crepes.

3. Cook potatoes in the oil in large skillet over medium heat, stirring occasionally, about 4 minutes.

4. Add chicken, mushrooms, green pepper, onion, salt, ground pepper and garlic powder to potatoes; cook 2 to 3 minutes longer.

5. Add wine to chicken mixture; cook until wine evaporates, 1 to 2 minutes longer. Remove from heat.

6. Heat oven to 350°F (180°C).

7. Spoon about ¼ cup (60 mL) of the chicken mixture evenly across center of each crepe. Fold over one side of each crepe, covering most of filling. Fold over opposite side, overlapping first fold. Repeat until all crepes are folded.

8. Place 6 finished crepes in each prepared baking dish. Pour ¾ cup (180 mL) remaining Salsa evenly over crepes in each dish. Cover dishes with aluminum foil. Bake until crepes are hot, 10 to 15 minutes.

9. Uncover dishes and arrange two strips cheese lengthwise over each crepe. Bake until cheese melts, about 2 minutes longer. Serve hot.

Tomato Wine Salsa

Makes about 2 cups (500 mL)

1 can (8 ounces or 225 g) tomato sauce
¾ cup (180 mL) hot water
½ cup (125 mL) dry red wine
⅓ cup (80 mL) tomato paste
2 teaspoons (10 mL) olive oil
1 clove garlic, cut into halves
⅛ teaspoon (0.5 mL) salt
⅛ teaspoon (0.5 mL) sugar
⅛ teaspoon (0.5 mL) pepper
⅛ teaspoon (0.5 mL) dried basil leaves

1. Blend all ingredients in 2-quart (2 L) saucepan.

2. Cook over high heat until mixture boils. Reduce heat to low; cover and simmer 15 minutes. Remove and discard garlic.

Crepes

Makes 12

2   eggs
½   teaspoon (2 mL) salt
1¼   cups (310 mL) all-purpose
      flour
1½   cups (375 mL) milk
2   tablespoons (30 mL) butter
      or margarine, melted
      Butter or margarine, at
      room temperature

1. Beat eggs and salt in medium bowl with whisk or electric mixer until well blended; gradually beat in flour alternately with milk. Stir melted butter into egg mixture. Cover and refrigerate batter at least 1 hour.

2. Brush 8-inch (20 cm) crepe pan or skillet lightly with room temperature butter. Heat pan over medium-high heat until just hot enough to sizzle a drop of water. For each crepe, pour about ¼ cup (60 mL) of the batter into pan, tipping and tilting pan to move batter quickly over bottom. Cook until crepe is light brown on bottom, about 1 minute. Turn crepe to brown other side, if desired. Remove crepe from pan and place on waxed paper.

3. Brush pan with additional butter as needed. Repeat cooking procedure until all crepes are cooked. Stack crepes between waxed paper until ready to use.* Fill warm crepes as desired.

*Note: Crepes can be wrapped in plastic and frozen up to 1 month. Thaw before using.

Chicken Liver Omelet

Makes 2 servings

8   ounces (225 g) chicken
      livers
3   tablespoons (45 mL) butter
      or margarine
1   teaspoon (5 mL) salt
¼   teaspoon (1 mL) ground
      pepper
      Pinch ground cumin
      Pinch garlic powder
3   tablespoons (45 mL) finely
      chopped onion
1   tablespoon (15 mL) finely
      chopped green pepper
3   eggs
4   thin slices tomato
      Thin green pepper rings, if
      desired
      Ripe olives, if desired

To turn a Sunday brunch into a special occasion, serve this delicate omelet that envelopes a tasty filling of sautéed chicken livers.

1. Remove and discard fat and white tissue from livers. Cut livers into bite-size pieces.

2. Melt 2 tablespoons (30 mL) of the butter in medium skillet over medium heat; add livers, ½ teaspoon (2 mL) of the salt, ⅛ teaspoon (0.5 mL) of the ground pepper, the cumin and garlic powder. Cook, stirring occasionally, 4 minutes. Add onion and chopped green pepper to liver mixture; cook 2 to 3 minutes longer. Remove from heat; cover and keep warm.

3. Combine eggs, remaining ½ teaspoon (2 mL) salt and ⅛ teaspoon (0.5 mL) pepper in small bowl; beat lightly.

4. Melt remaining 1 tablespoon (15 mL) butter in 9-inch (23 cm) omelet pan over medium heat until just hot enough to sizzle a drop of water; pour in egg mixture. With inverted pancake turner, push cooked portions of egg at edges toward center so uncooked portions flow to bottom; tilt pan as necessary so uncooked eggs can flow. Slide pan rapidly back and forth over heat to keep omelet sliding freely. Cook until eggs are set, 2 to 3 minutes.

5. Arrange liver mixture across center third of omelet; top with tomato slices. Fold both sides of omelet over to cover livers and tomato; carefully turn omelet onto serving plate. Garnish with green pepper rings and ripe olives.

Chicken Kibbe

Makes 15 pieces

¾ cup (180 mL) bulgur or cracked wheat
Cold water
Chicken Filling (recipe follows)
1 pound (450 g) lean lamb or sirloin, ground twice
½ cup (125 mL) finely chopped onion
1 teaspoon (5 mL) salt
½ teaspoon (2 mL) pepper
½ cup (125 mL) ice water
½ cup (125 mL) butter or margarine, melted

Kibbe is a national dish of the Syrians and Lebanese. In this version, a chicken filling is sandwiched between two layers of a ground lamb and cracked wheat mixture.

1. Place bulgur in medium bowl. Add enough cold water to reach a level 1 inch (2.5 cm) above the bulgur; let stand 1 hour. Drain bulgur.

2. Prepare Chicken Filling.

3. Heat oven to 400°F (200°C).

4. Combine bulgur, lamb, onion, salt and pepper in large bowl; mix thoroughly.

5. Grind mixture through fine blade of food grinder, slowly adding ice water as the meat is being ground.

6. Pat half of the lamb mixture evenly into greased 11x7x2-inch (28x18x5 cm) baking dish. Spread Chicken Filling evenly over lamb mixture in dish; press down firmly. Cover evenly with remaining lamb mixture; press down firmly.

7. Using sharp knife, cut diagonal lines, if desired, across top to form diamond pattern; drizzle evenly with butter.

8. Bake until top is golden, 15 to 20 minutes. Cut into 2-inch (5 cm) squares or diamonds. Serve hot or cold.

Chicken Filling

Makes about 2 cups (500 mL)

3 tablespoons (45 mL) butter or margarine
1½ cups (375 mL) ground or shredded uncooked chicken
¾ cup (180 mL) finely chopped onion
1 tablespoon (15 mL) minced fresh parsley
¼ teaspoon (1 mL) salt
⅛ teaspoon (0.5 mL) pepper

1. Melt butter in medium skillet over medium heat; add chicken and onion. Cook, stirring frequently, until chicken is golden, 5 to 8 minutes. Remove from heat; stir in remaining ingredients.

Swedish Cutlets

Makes 6 cutlets

These sautéed chicken and mushroom patties are served with a creamy dill-flavored sauce.

6	tablespoons (90 mL) butter or margarine
3	cups (750 mL) shredded cooked chicken
1	can (4 ounces or 115 g) mushrooms, drained and minced
2	tablespoons (30 mL) finely chopped onion
2	tablespoons (30 mL) all-purpose flour
¾	cup (180 mL) chicken broth
1	teaspoon (5 mL) salt
¼	teaspoon (1 mL) pepper
3	egg yolks
½	cup (125 mL) all-purpose flour
1	egg, slightly beaten
¾	cup (180 mL) fine dry bread crumbs
2	tablespoons (30 mL) vegetable oil
	Creamy Dill Sauce (recipe follows)

1. Melt 2 tablespoons (30 mL) of the butter in 2-quart (2 L) saucepan over medium heat; add chicken, mushrooms and onion. Cook until chicken is golden, 5 to 8 minutes.

2. Stir the 2 tablespoons (30 mL) flour into chicken mixture; cook 1 minute. Blend broth gradually into flour mixture; stir in salt and pepper. Reduce heat; cook until liquid evaporates, 7 to 10 minutes. Remove from heat.

3. Beat egg yolks lightly in small bowl; slowly blend ⅓ cup (80 mL) of the chicken mixture into beaten yolks, stirring constantly. Stir yolk mixture slowly into chicken mixture. Cover and refrigerate until mixture is firm, at least 3 hours or overnight.

4. Shape mixture into 6 cutlets each about 4½x2½ inches (11.5x6.5 cm), dipping cutlets lightly in ½ cup (125 mL) flour as necessary to help shape them.

5. Dip cutlets in beaten egg to coat both sides; dip in bread crumbs, pressing to coat both sides well. Arrange cutlets on waxed paper-lined plate. Refrigerate 20 to 30 minutes.

6. Heat remaining 4 tablespoons (60 mL) butter and the oil in large skillet over medium heat; add cutlets. Cook until cutlets are golden, about 5 minutes on each side. Keep cutlets warm in 200°F (90°C) oven until ready to serve.

7. Prepare Creamy Dill Sauce. Serve cutlets with sauce.

Creamy Dill Sauce

Makes 1⅓ cups (330 mL)

2	tablespoons (30 mL) butter or margarine
2	tablespoons (30 mL) all-purpose flour
2	cups (500 mL) half and half
1	tablespoon (15 mL) white wine vinegar
2	tablespoons (30 mL) minced fresh or 2 teaspoons (10 mL) dried dill weed
1	teaspoon (5 mL) sugar
½	teaspoon (2 mL) salt
¼	teaspoon (1 mL) white pepper

1. Melt butter in 2-quart (2 L) saucepan over medium heat; stir in flour to make smooth paste. Cook 1 minute.

2. Blend half and half gradually into flour mixture. Cook, stirring constantly, until thick, about 5 minutes. Remove from heat.

3. Stir remaining ingredients into sauce. Serve hot.

Shrimp and Chicken in Brioches

Makes about 6 servings

Petites Brioches (recipe
follows)
6 tablespoons (90 mL) butter
or margarine
2 large whole chicken
breasts, deboned,
skinned and cut into
1x¼-inch (2.5x0.5 cm)
strips
¾ teaspoon (4 mL) salt
¼ teaspoon (1 mL) pepper
¼ cup (60 mL) finely chopped
celery
¼ cup (60 mL) finely chopped
onion
3 tablespoons (45 mL) all-
purpose flour
2 cups (500 mL) milk
¼ cup (60 mL) Madeira wine
or dry sherry
1 teaspoon (5 mL) sugar
½ teaspoon (2 mL) poultry
seasoning
¼ teaspoon (1 mL) dried
summer savory leaves
Pinch ground nutmeg
8 ounces (225 g) cooked
deveined shrimp

*Add an elegant touch to any special occasion with this superb
combination of shrimp and chicken served in Petites Brioches. A medley
of fresh fruit and a chilled white wine are all that are needed to complete
the menu.*

1. Prepare Petites Brioches several hours or the day before serving.
Reserve.

2. Melt butter in large skillet over medium heat; add chicken, salt and
pepper. Cook, stirring occasionally, until chicken is done, 8 to 10 minutes.
Remove chicken and reserve.

3. Cook celery and onion in pan drippings until onion is transparent,
about 3 minutes.

4. Stir flour into onion mixture; cook, stirring constantly, 1 minute. Add
milk gradually to flour mixture, stirring constantly; stir in Madeira, sugar,
poultry seasoning, savory and nutmeg. Cook, stirring constantly, until
mixture is thick, about 5 minutes.

5. Add chicken and shrimp to milk mixture; cook until mixture boils.
Remove from heat.

6. Slice top cap off each brioche; hollow out center of each brioche. Fill
each brioche with about ¼ cup (60 mL) of the chicken mixture. Replace
cap. Serve hot.

Petites Brioches

Makes 18

¼ cup (60 mL) warm water
(105° to 115°F or
41° to 46°C)
1 package (¼ ounce or 7 g)
active dry yeast
3½ cups (875 mL) all-purpose
flour
½ cup (125 mL) milk, scalded
and cooled
½ cup (125 mL) butter or
margarine, at room
temperature
3 whole eggs plus 1 egg yolk
continued

1. Combine water and yeast in large mixer bowl; stir until yeast dissolves.

2. Add 2 cups (500 mL) of the flour, the milk, butter, whole eggs and egg
yolk, 2 tablespoons (30 mL) of the sugar and the salt to yeast mixture.
Beat on medium speed of electric mixer 3 minutes; scrape sides of bowl.

3. Add remaining 1½ cups (375 mL) flour to batter; beat until smooth,
about 2 minutes longer. Cover loosely with plastic wrap. Let stand in
warm place (85°F or 30°C) until doubled, 1½ to 2 hours.

4. Stir down dough. Cover bowl tightly and refrigerate overnight.

5. Place dough on lightly floured surface. Divide dough into 4 equal
pieces. Set aside 1 piece of the dough; divide each remaining piece into 6
pieces, making a total of 18 pieces.

Petites Brioches (continued)

3   tablespoons (45 mL) sugar
½   teaspoon (2 mL) salt
1   egg white

6. Form each piece into a smooth ball and place in well-greased small brioche mold or large muffin cup.

7. Divide reserved piece of dough into 18 small pieces. Shape each into a tear-drop shape. Make an identation with back of a spoon into center top of each ball of dough in brioche molds; insert tear-drop shaped dough into each indentation.

8. Cover loosely with plastic wrap. Let stand in warm place until doubled, about 1 hour.

9. Heat oven to 375°F (190°C).

10. Beat egg white and remaining 1 tablespoon (15 mL) of the sugar with fork; brush each brioche with egg mixture. Bake until brioches are golden, 15 to 20 minutes. Remove immediately from molds; cool on wire rack.

Makes 4

Tortilla Pizzas

2   tablespoons (30 mL) butter
        or margarine
2   cups (500 mL) chopped
        cooked chicken
1   teaspoon (5 mL) dried
        oregano leaves
½   teaspoon (2 mL) salt
⅛   teaspoon (0.5 mL) ground
        pepper
        Vegetable oil
4   large corn tortillas
        (10 inches or 25 cm
        in diameter each)
8   tablespoons (125 mL)
        chopped tomato
8   tablespoons (125 mL) thinly
        sliced green onions
4   tablespoons (60 mL)
        chopped green pepper
8   tablespoons (125 mL) pizza
        sauce
1   cup (250 mL) shredded
        Cheddar or mozzarella
        cheese (4 ounces or
        115 g)
        Chile peppers, if desired

These festive Mexican-style pizzas will be popular with everyone, especially teenagers.

1. Heat oven to 375°F (190°C).

2. Melt butter in 10-inch (25 cm) skillet over medium heat; add chicken, oregano, salt and ground pepper. Cook chicken mixture in the butter until golden, 3 to 5 minutes. Remove chicken from skillet, place in bowl and reserve.

3. Pour oil into the skillet until it reaches a level of ¼ inch (0.5 cm); heat oil over medium-high heat. Cook a tortilla in the oil until tortilla is crisp, about 1 minute. Remove tortilla from skillet, drain on paper toweling and place on large cookie sheet. Repeat to cook remaining tortillas.

4. Spoon ¼ of the chicken mixture evenly over each tortilla. Top each with 2 tablespoons (30 mL) tomato, 2 tablespoons (30 mL) onion, 1 tablespoon (15 mL) green pepper, 2 tablespoons (30 mL) pizza sauce and ¼ cup (60 mL) cheese. Bake until cheese melts, about 5 minutes. Garnish with chile peppers. Serve hot.

Alpine Chicken and Pork

Makes 4 to 6 servings

Cheese Noodle Cups or
Vermouth French Toast
(recipes follow)
- ¼ cup (60 mL) butter or margarine
- 6 chicken thighs, deboned, skinned and cut into 1x¼-inch (2.5x0.5 cm) strips
- 8 ounces (225 g) boneless lean pork, cut into 1x¼-inch (2.5x0.5 cm) strips
- 1½ cups (375 mL) apple juice
- 1 teaspoon (5 mL) salt
- ¼ teaspoon (1 mL) dried rosemary leaves, crushed
- ¼ teaspoon (1 mL) ground mace
- ½ teaspoon (2 mL) cornstarch
- 1 tablespoon (15 mL) water
- ⅔ cup (160 mL) diced apple
- ¼ cup (60 mL) shredded Swiss cheese (1 ounce or 30 g)
- 1 cup (250 mL) sour cream

The distinctive flavor of apple enhances the cheesy sour cream sauce used in this delightful luncheon entrée. A leafy Boston lettuce salad is a good accompaniment.

1. Prepare Cheese Noodle Cups with Swiss cheese or prepare Vermouth French Toast; reserve.

2. Melt butter in large skillet over medium heat. Cook chicken and pork in the butter, stirring occasionally, until golden, about 8 minutes.

3. Add apple juice, salt, rosemary and mace to chicken mixture; cook until mixture boils. Reduce heat; simmer until pork is tender, about 45 minutes.

4. Blend cornstarch and water in small bowl; stir into chicken-apple juice mixture. Cook 1 minute.

5. Add apple to chicken mixture; cook 2 minutes longer. Add cheese to chicken mixture; cook, stirring constantly, until cheese melts.

6. Blend sour cream into chicken mixture. Cook just until hot throughout. Do not boil.

7. Pour chicken mixture into Cheese Noodle Cups or over Vermouth French Toast. Serve hot.

Cheese Noodle Cups

Makes 8

- 1 can (5 ounces or 140 g) chow mein noodles (2½ cups or 625 mL)
- 1 cup (250 mL) shredded Swiss, colby, Monterey Jack, brick or Cheddar cheese (4 ounces or 250 mL)
- 1 egg white, slightly beaten

1. Heat oven to 300°F (150°C).

2. Place all ingredients in medium bowl; mix well.

3. Press mixture firmly over bottom and completely up sides of 8 medium-size greased muffin cups. Bake until noodle cups are golden, 12 to 15 minutes. Remove carefully from cups; cool on wire rack.

Vermouth French Toast

3   eggs, slightly beaten
½   cup (125 mL) milk
¼   cup (60 mL) sweet
      vermouth
½   teaspoon (2 mL) salt
1   teaspoon (5 mL) sugar
6   to 8 slices day-old white
      or whole wheat bread

1. Heat oven to 450°F (230°C).

2. Combine eggs, milk, vermouth, salt and sugar in shallow dish or pie plate.

3. Dip bread into egg mixture, turning to coat both sides. Arrange bread on well-greased cookie sheet.

4. Bake until slices are golden on the bottoms, 8 to 10 minutes. Turn slices over; bake until golden on bottoms, 8 to 10 minutes longer.

Spinach Quiche

1   medium leek
      Water
¼   cup (60 mL) butter or
      margarine
2   cups (500 mL) finely
      chopped cooked chicken
½   package (10-ounce or
      285 g size) frozen
      chopped spinach or
      broccoli, cooked and
      drained
1   10-inch (25 cm) pie crust,
      unbaked
1   tablespoon (15 mL) all-
      purpose flour
1½ cups (375 mL) shredded
      Swiss cheese (6 ounces or
      170 g)
4   eggs
1½ cups (375 mL) half and
      half or evaporated milk
2   tablespoons (30 mL)
      brandy
½   teaspoon (2 mL) salt
¼   teaspoon (1 mL) pepper
¼   teaspoon (1 mL) ground
      nutmeg

This quiche is exceptionally enticing. The creamy custard is richly flavored with chicken, spinach, Swiss cheese and a splash of brandy.

1. Heat oven to 375°F (190°C).

2. Cut leek in half lengthwise; wash and trim, leaving 2 to 3 inches (5 to 8 cm) of the green top intact. Cut leek crosswise into thin slices.

3. Place leek in small saucepan; add enough water to cover. Cook over high heat until water boils; reduce heat and simmer 5 minutes. Drain and reserve leek.

4. Melt butter in large skillet over medium heat; add chicken. Cook until chicken is golden, about 5 minutes.

5. Add spinach and leek to chicken mixture; cook 1 to 2 minutes longer. Remove from heat.

6. Sprinkle chicken mixture into pie crust. Sprinkle flour and cheese over chicken mixture.

7. Beat eggs lightly in medium bowl; blend in remaining ingredients. Pour egg mixture over cheese.

8. Bake until knife inserted in center comes out clean, 35 to 40 minutes. Let stand 5 minutes before serving. Serve hot or cold.

Festive Creamed Chicken

Makes 8 servings

Vermouth French Toast or
    Petites Brioches (see
    Index for page numbers)
⅓ cup (80 mL) chopped green
    pepper
¼ cup (60 mL) water
⅓ cup (80 mL) butter or
    margarine
3 tablespoons (45 mL) all-
    purpose flour
1 teaspoon (5 mL) salt
¾ teaspoon (4 mL) paprika
⅛ teaspoon (0.5 mL) white
    pepper
1½ cups (375 mL) chicken
    broth
1½ cups (375 mL) half and half
½ cup (125 mL) dry sherry
4 egg yolks
4 cups (1 L) chopped cooked
    chicken
2 cans (8 ounces or 225 g
    each) mushroom stems
    and pieces, drained
1 jar (2 ounces or 60 g)
    chopped pimientos,
    drained

For a memorable meal, serve this luscious creamed chicken poured over elegant French toast or tucked inside golden, egg-rich individual brioches.

1. Prepare Vermouth French Toast or Petites Brioches. Cut caps off brioches; hollow out centers. Reserve brioche bottoms and caps.

2. Place green pepper and water in small saucepan; cook over medium-high heat until water boils. Cook until green pepper is soft, about 3 minutes; drain, reserving green pepper.

3. Melt butter in 3-quart (3 L) saucepan over medium heat; add flour, salt, paprika, and white pepper. Cook, stirring constantly, until bubbly; blend in broth, half and half and sherry. Cook, stirring constantly, until thick, about 5 minutes. Remove from heat.

4. Beat egg yolks lightly in small bowl. Slowly blend about ¼ cup (60 mL) of the hot half and half mixture into egg yolks, stirring constantly. Stir egg mixture slowly into half and half mixture in saucepan; add remaining ingredients. Cook, stirring occasionally, until mixture bubbles.

5. Serve over Vermouth French Toast or in hollowed-out brioches. Replace brioche caps. Serve hot.

Creamed Luau Chicken
Prepare as directed for Festive Creamed Chicken substituting 1 can (16 ounces or 450 g) well-drained pineapple chunks for mushrooms.

Chicken Terrapin
Prepare as directed for Festive Creamed Chicken, reducing chicken to 3 cups (750 mL). Just before serving, add 4 or 5 chopped hard-cooked eggs and ⅓ cup (80 mL) chopped ripe olives.

Creamed Rarebit-Style Chicken
Prepare as directed for Festive Creamed Chicken, reducing chicken to 3 cups (750 mL). Just before serving, add ⅔ cup (160 mL) shredded Cheddar, colby or American Cheese. Stir until cheese melts.

Eggplant Chicken Strata

Makes 4 servings

1 medium eggplant
1 teaspoon (5 mL) salt
½ cup (125 mL) all-purpose flour
  Vegetable oil
2 tablespoons (30 mL) butter or margarine
1 large whole chicken breast, deboned, skinned and cut into 1x¼-inch (2.5x0.5 cm) strips
1 small onion, thinly sliced
⅓ cup (80 mL) cubed green pepper
1 small clove garlic, pressed
1 teaspoon (5 mL) minced fresh or dried parsley
⅛ teaspoon (0.5 mL) dried oregano leaves
  Pinch cayenne pepper
  Pinch ground nutmeg
  Yogurt Sauce (recipe follows)
1 tomato, cut into 8 wedges, if desired

This Eastern Mediterranean-style dish is ideal for those seeking the unusual. Strips of chicken and cubes of green pepper are delicately seasoned, sautéed and sandwiched between circles of sautéed eggplant. A creamy yogurt sauce completes the dish.

1. Pare eggplant; cut crosswise into 8 slices ¼-inch (0.5 cm) thick each. Sprinkle slices with ½ teaspoon (2 mL) of the salt; dip in flour to coat both sides.

2. Pour oil into large skillet to a level of ½ inch (1.5 cm). Heat oil over medium heat until hot; add eggplant slices. Cook until slices are golden, 3 to 4 minutes on each side. Drain slices on paper toweling.

3. Melt butter in small skillet over medium heat; add chicken. Cook, stirring occasionally, until golden, about 8 minutes.

4. Add onion, green pepper, garlic, parsley, remaining ½ teaspoon (2 mL) salt, the oregano, cayenne pepper and nutmeg to chicken mixture. Cook, stirring occasionally, until chicken is done, 5 to 7 minutes longer.

5. Meanwhile, prepare Yogurt Sauce.

6. Place 1 eggplant slice on each of 4 serving plates. Spoon ¼ of the chicken mixture over each eggplant slice; top with 1 tablespoon (15 mL) of the yogurt sauce. Cover with remaining eggplant slices. Pour scant ½ cup (125 mL) remaining Yogurt Sauce over each serving. Garnish with tomato wedges. Serve immediately.

Yogurt Sauce

Makes 2 cups (500 mL)

2 tablespoons (30 mL) butter or margarine
2 tablespoons (30 mL) all-purpose flour
1 cup (250 mL) milk
1 cup (250 mL) plain yogurt, at room temperature
  Pinch ground nutmeg

1. Melt butter in 1-quart (1 L) saucepan over medium heat; stir in flour to make a smooth paste. Cook 1 minute. Blend milk gradually into flour mixture; cook, stirring constantly, until thick, 5 to 7 minutes.

2. Stir yogurt in small bowl with fork until creamy; blend in ¼ cup (60 mL) of the milk mixture. Slowly pour yogurt mixture, stirring constantly, into hot milk mixture.

3. Cook over low heat just until yogurt is warm. Remove from heat; stir in nutmeg.

Chicken Hoppel Poppel

2	tablespoons (30 mL) butter or margarine
1	tablespoon (15 mL) vegetable oil
½	cup (125 mL) finely chopped cooked chicken
¼	cup (60 mL) finely chopped corned beef
1	cup (250 mL) shredded uncooked potato
1	tablespoon (15 mL) finely chopped onion
¼	teaspoon (1 mL) salt
⅛	teaspoon (0.5 mL) pepper
3	eggs, beaten
1	to 2 tablespoons (15 to 30 mL) shredded Cheddar or colby cheese, if desired
1	teaspoon (5 mL) water

Hoppel Poppel, which traditionally is an open-faced omelet flavored with potato and onion, is believed to have originated in the famous delicatessens of New York City. In this version, chicken and corned beef are added to the basic omelet.

1. Heat butter and oil in large skillet over medium heat; add chicken, corned beef, potato, onion, salt and pepper. Cook over low heat, stirring frequently, about 3 minutes.

2. Continue cooking, pressing mixture firmly with spatula, until bottom crust is golden, about 5 minutes longer. Cut chicken mixture into quarters and invert; cook 2 minutes longer.

3. Pour eggs over chicken mixture; cook until eggs are almost set, 3 to 5 minutes.

4. Turn Hoppel Poppel over by inverting onto a plate and then sliding back into skillet; sprinkle with cheese and water.

5. Cover and cook until cheese melts, about 1 minute. Slide onto warm serving plate. Serve hot.

Chicken Patties with Celery Sauce

	Celery Sauce (recipe follows), if desired
2	eggs
2	tablespoons (30 mL) evaporated milk or cream
½	teaspoon (2 mL) dried parsley flakes
⅛	teaspoon (0.5 mL) salt
⅛	teaspoon (0.5 mL) pepper
⅛	teaspoon (0.5 mL) dried oregano leaves
1	cup (250 mL) shredded cooked chicken
6	tablespoons (90 mL) fine dry bread crumbs
2	teaspoons (10 mL) butter or margarine
2	teaspoons (10 mL) vegetable oil

Here's a delicious entrée that can be served plain or with an interesting celery sauce. Served with a green vegetable, it makes a nice luncheon.

1. Prepare Celery Sauce.

2. Combine 1 of the eggs, 1 tablespoon (15 mL) of the milk, the parsley, salt, pepper and oregano in small bowl; beat until frothy.

3. Add chicken and 2 tablespoons (30 mL) of the bread crumbs to egg mixture; mix well. Shape chicken mixture into 4 flat patties; reserve.

4. Beat the remaining egg with remaining 1 tablespoon (15 mL) milk in shallow pan. Dip patties in egg mixture, coating both sides; dip in remaining bread crumbs, pressing to coat well.

5. Heat butter and oil in large skillet over medium heat. Cook patties in butter mixture until golden, about 5 minutes on each side. Serve with Celery Sauce.

Makes about 1 cup (250 mL) ## Celery Sauce

---

2   tablespoons (30 mL) butter
    or margarine
⅓   cup (80 mL) finely chopped
    celery
1   tablespoon (15 mL) finely
    chopped onion
1½ tablespoons (22 mL) all-
    purpose flour
1   cup (250 mL) milk
½   teaspoon (2 mL) salt
⅛   teaspoon (0.5 mL) pepper

1. Melt butter in 1-quart (1 L) saucepan over medium heat; add celery and onion. Cook until onion is transparent, about 3 minutes.

2. Add flour to celery mixture; cook 1 minute. Blend milk gradually into flour mixture; add salt and pepper. Cook, stirring constantly, until thick, 5 to 7 minutes. Keep warm until ready to serve.

Makes 4 to 6 servings # Couscous Casbah

---

2   cups (500 mL) bulgur or
    cracked wheat
    Water
¼   cup (60 mL) butter or
    margarine
2   tablespoons (30 mL)
    vegetable oil
3   cups (750 mL) diced
    uncooked chicken
½   cup (125 mL) chopped
    onion
3   cups (750 mL) chicken
    broth
1   cup (250 mL) cubed peeled
    fresh or drained canned
    tomatoes
2   teaspoons (10 mL) salt
¼   teaspoon (1 mL) ground
    turmeric
⅛   teaspoon (0.5 mL) cayenne
    pepper
    Pinch ground allspice
¼   cup (60 mL) diced green
    pepper
¼   cup (60 mL) diced carrot
1   cup (250 mL) frozen peas
    Minced fresh parsley

This is a popular dish in several North African countries. There are many variations of this cracked wheat entrée, including this one which features diced chicken, fresh tomatoes and other vegetables simmered in broth.

1. Rinse bulgur with water; drain well and reserve.

2. Heat butter and oil in 5-quart (5 L) Dutch oven over medium heat; add chicken. Cook, stirring occasionally, until chicken is golden, 10 minutes; add onion. Cook until onion is soft, about 3 minutes.

3. Add broth, tomatoes, salt, turmeric, cayenne pepper and allspice to chicken mixture. Cook until broth boils.

4. Stir bulgur, green pepper and carrot into broth mixture; heat to boiling. Reduce heat; cover and simmer 10 minutes.

5. Add peas to chicken mixture; cover and cook until all water is absorbed, 10 to 15 minutes longer.

6. Place Couscous in serving bowl or press firmly into a greased 2-quart (2 L) mold. Place serving platter over mold; invert and remove mold. Serve hot, garnished with parsley.

Pickled Chicken Bolivian

Makes 4 to 6 servings

1   small onion, cut into halves
1   broiling/frying chicken
      (about 3 pounds or
      1350 g), cut into serving
      pieces
2   thin lemon slices
3   tablespoons (45 mL) mixed
      whole pickling spice
2   teaspoons (10 mL) crushed
      red pepper
1   teaspoon (5 mL) salt
1½ cups (375 mL) white wine
      vinegar
¼   cup (60 mL) olive or
      vegetable oil
¼   cup (60 mL) water
      Prepared horseradish, if
      desired

This is an interesting way to prepare chicken for cold luncheon plates, sandwiches or buffet tables. The chicken is simmered in spiced vinegar, refrigerated and cut into thin slices for serving.

1. Place all ingredients except horseradish in 5-quart (5 L) Dutch oven. Cook over high heat until liquid boils. Reduce heat to low; cover and simmer until chicken is tender, about 1 hour.

2. Remove chicken from Dutch oven; cool to lukewarm. Remove meat from chicken, discarding skin and bones. Cover chicken and refrigerate about 3 hours.

3. Slice chicken thinly and arrange on serving plate. Serve with horseradish.

Surprise Potatoes

Makes 4 servings

2   large baking potatoes
      (about 6 inches or 15 cm
      long each), baked
4   tablespoons (60 mL) butter
      or margarine, at room
      temperature
2   large whole chicken breasts,
      deboned and skinned
¾   teaspoon (4 mL) dried
      Italian herb seasoning
      leaves
½   teaspoon (2 mL) salt
⅛   teaspoon (0.5) pepper
8   tablespoons (125 mL)
      shredded American,
      Cheddar, colby, brick or
      Monterey Jack cheese
      (2 ounces or 60 g)

Hollowed-out baked potato shells are filled with layers of sautéed chicken and shredded cheese, then popped into the oven to melt the cheese.

1. Heat oven to 350°F (180°C).

2. Cut each baked potato lengthwise into halves; scoop out centers, leaving ½-inch (1.5 cm) border. Reserve pulp for another use. Brush halves with 2 tablespoons (30 mL) of the butter. Arrange potatoes on cookie sheet and place in preheated oven. Bake until shells are hot, 5 to 7 minutes.

3. While potatoes are baking, cut chicken breasts into halves. Flatten each half by pounding between two pieces of waxed paper. Melt remaining 2 tablespoons (30 mL) butter in large skillet over medium heat; add chicken, herbs, salt and pepper. Cook until chicken is golden, 3 to 4 minutes on each side. Cut chicken into ½-inch (1.5 cm) strips. Sprinkle 1 tablespoon (15 mL) of the cheese into each potato half; top each with ¼ of the chicken and 1 tablespoon (15 mL) cheese. Bake until cheese melts, about 5 minutes longer. Serve hot.

Main Dishes

Main dishes for all occasions are included
in this chapter. You'll find sophisticated entrées
for formal dining, easy dishes for
casual family eating, ethnic favorites, and even
some recipes for outdoor grilling.

Chicken Cutlets Celebration

Makes 6 to 8 servings

1   can (29 ounces or 830 g) peach halves, packed in syrup
½   package (20-ounce or 570 g size) frozen whole unsweetened or 1 pint (500 mL) fresh strawberries
2   tablespoons (30 mL) sugar
4   large whole chicken breasts, deboned, skinned and split lengthwise into halves
½   teaspoon (2 mL) salt
⅛   teaspoon (0.5 mL) pepper
4   tablespoons (60 mL) butter or margarine
2   tablespoons (30 mL) cornstarch
¼   cup (60 mL) peach preserves
1   stick cinnamon (about 2 inches or 5 cm long)
4   whole cloves
¼   cup (60 mL) brandy
    Hot cooked rice

This festive and attractive party dish features golden chicken breasts, peaches and strawberries in a spicy fruit-flavored sauce. Just before serving, flaming brandy is poured over the dish.

1. Drain peaches, reserving syrup; add enough water to syrup to measure 2 cups (500 mL). Reserve.

2. Sprinkle strawberries with sugar; reserve.

3. Flatten chicken by pounding lightly between 2 pieces of waxed paper until ¼ inch (0.5 cm) thick; sprinkle with salt and pepper.

4. Melt 2 tablespoons (30 mL) of the butter in large skillet over medium heat; add 4 of the chicken cutlets. Cook until chicken is light brown, 3 to 4 minutes on each side. Reduce heat; cook until chicken is done, 8 to 10 minutes longer. Remove from skillet; keep warm in 200°F (90°C) oven.

5. Melt remaining 2 tablespoons (30 mL) butter in skillet; repeat procedure to cook remaining chicken. Remove chicken from skillet; keep warm.

6. Blend cornstarch with ¼ cup (60 mL) of the reserved juice mixture; stir into drippings in skillet. Cook, stirring constantly, about 1 minute. Blend remaining peach juice mixture gradually into cornstarch mixture; add preserves, cinnamon and cloves. Cook, stirring constantly, until thick, 2 to 3 minutes.

7. Add peaches to thickened mixture; heat to boiling. Boil 1 minute.

8. Add chicken and strawberries to peach mixture. Cook just until strawberries are hot, 1 to 2 minutes. (Do not overcook strawberries or they will become mushy.)

9. Heat brandy in small saucepan over medium heat just until warm. Carefully ignite brandy using long wood match. Pour brandy over chicken and sauce mixture; serve immediately over rice.

MAIN DISHES

Beer-Barbecued Chicken

Makes 4 servings

1 teaspoon (5 mL) Seasoned Salt (see Index for page number)
1 broiling/frying chicken (about 3 pounds or 1350 g), cut into serving pieces
1 can or bottle (12 ounces or 375 mL) beer
1 tablespoon (15 mL) dark brown sugar
1 tablespoon (15 mL) lemon juice
1 tablespoon (15 mL) vegetable oil
1 tablespoon (15 mL) dark molasses
⅛ teaspoon (0.5 mL) red pepper sauce

Ideal for patio parties and other outdoor cookouts, this robustly flavored chicken is basted with a marinade prepared with beer.

1. Prepare Seasoned Salt. Rub Seasoned Salt evenly over chicken. Arrange chicken in single layer in shallow 2-quart (2 L) baking dish.

2. Mix all remaining ingredients in small bowl; pour over chicken pieces. Cover and refrigerate at least 4 hours or overnight; turn chicken over several times during marinating.

3. Preheat coals in outdoor barbecue cooker according to manufacturer's directions.

4. Remove chicken from marinade, reserving marinade. Arrange chicken, skin-side up, on cooking rack 5 to 7 inches (13 to 18 cm) above hot coals. Cook until underside of chicken is dark brown, 20 to 25 minutes.

5. Brush chicken with marinade; turn chicken over and brush again with marinade. Cook until underside of chicken is dark brown, 20 to 25 minutes longer. Turn chicken over; continue cooking until chicken is fork tender, 5 to 10 minutes longer, brushing frequently with marinade. Serve hot or cold.

Chicken Wellington

Makes 4 servings

Pastry Dough (recipe follows)
2 large whole chicken breasts, deboned, skinned and split lengthwise into halves
½ teaspoon (2 mL) salt
⅛ teaspoon (0.5 mL) pepper
4 ounces (115 g) Monterey Jack or Swiss cheese, cut into ⅛-inch (0.5 cm) wide strips
2 thin slices boiled ham (about 1 ounce or 30 g each), cut into ⅛-inch (0.5 cm) wide strips
2 tablespoons (30 mL) butter or margarine
Cold water
1 egg yolk
1 tablespoon (15 mL) water
continued

For entertaining, try these boneless chicken breasts that are rolled around julienne strips of ham and cheese. They are sautéed, wrapped in pastry, baked until crisp and served with a light vegetable sauce.

1. Prepare Pastry Dough; refrigerate until ready to use.

2. Heat oven to 400°F (200°C).

3. Flatten chicken by pounding lightly between 2 pieces of waxed paper until ¼ inch (0.5 cm) thick; sprinkle with salt and pepper.

4. Place ¼ of the cheese and ham strips across center of each piece chicken. Carefully fold chicken so ham and cheese are completely enclosed; press edges firmly together. Secure with wooden pick.

5. Melt butter in large skillet over medium heat; add chicken. Cook until chicken is light brown, 4 to 5 minutes on each side. Remove chicken.

6. Divide Pastry Dough into 4 equal balls. Roll out each ball on lightly floured surface into rectangle large enough to wrap completely around one chicken piece. Place a chicken piece in center of dough and remove wooden pick. Fold pastry over chicken; trim off excess dough. Brush edges lightly with cold water and seal well; place seam-side down in greased 15½x10½x1-inch (39x26.5x2.5 cm) jelly-roll pan. Repeat procedure with remaining dough and chicken.

Chicken Wellington *(continued)*

2   cups (500 mL) Bordelaise
    Sauce (see Index for page
    number)

7. Beat egg yolk and 1 tablespoon (15 mL) water in small bowl; carefully brush mixture over each pastry. Bake until pastry is golden and crisp, about 40 minutes.

8. Meanwhile, prepare Bordelaise Sauce. Serve chicken hot with sauce.

Pastry Dough

3   cups (750 mL) all-purpose
    flour
¾   teaspoon (4 mL) salt
¾   cup (180 mL) shortening
8   to 10 tablespoons (125 to
    155 mL) cold water

1. Mix flour and salt in large bowl; cut in ½ cup (125 mL) of the shortening until mixture resembles cornmeal. Cut in remaining ¼ cup (60 mL) shortening until pieces are the size of peas.

2. Sprinkle water, 1 tablespoon (15 mL) at a time, over flour mixture; mix just until dough holds together. Shape dough into ball; cover and refrigerate 30 minutes before rolling.

Ginger Peachy Barbecued Chicken

Makes 4 servings

1   can (29 ounces or 830 g)
    peach halves, packed in
    syrup
½   cup (125 mL) peach
    preserves
¼   cup (60 mL) butter or
    margarine
1   tablespoon (15 mL) cider
    vinegar
1   teaspoon (5 mL) instant
    minced onion
1   teaspoon (5 mL) salt
1   teaspoon (5 mL) dry
    mustard
1   teaspoon (5 mL) ground
    ginger
½   teaspoon (2 mL) whole
    cloves
¼   teaspoon (1 mL) pepper
1   broiling/frying chicken
    (about 3 pounds or
    1350 g), cut into serving
    pieces
⅛   teaspoon (0.5 mL) ground
    cinnamon

This outdoor barbecued chicken is flavored with a peach marinating and basting sauce.

1. Drain peaches, reserving peaches and syrup. Place syrup in 1-quart (1 L) saucepan; add preserves, butter, vinegar, onion, salt, mustard, ginger, cloves and pepper. Cook over medium heat, stirring constantly, until mixture boils. Remove from heat; cool about 10 minutes.

2. Arrange chicken in single layer in shallow 2-quart (2 L) baking dish. Pour syrup mixture over chicken; turn pieces over. Cover with plastic wrap and refrigerate at least 4 hours or overnight. Turn chicken over several times during marinating.

3. Preheat coals in outdoor barbecue cooker according to manufacturer's directions.

4. Remove chicken from marinade, reserving marinade. Arrange chicken skin-side up, on cooking rack 5 to 7 inches (13 to 18 cm) above hot coals. Cook until underside of chicken is dark brown, 20 to 25 minutes.

5. Brush chicken with marinade; turn chicken over and brush again with marinade. Cook until underside of chicken is dark brown, 20 to 25 minutes longer. Turn chicken over; continue cooking until chicken is fork tender, 5 to 10 minutes longer, brushing frequently with marinade.

6. During last 15 minutes of cooking, place reserved peaches on piece of heavy-duty aluminum foil; sprinkle with cinnamon. Close foil tightly; place on cooking rack over hot coals until peaches are hot, about 15 minutes. Serve chicken hot with peaches.

MAIN DISHES

Crispy Baked Chicken

1 broiling/frying chicken (about 3 pounds or 1350 g), cut into serving pieces
½ cup (125 mL) water
1 tablespoon (15 mL) Seasoned Salt (recipe follows)
¾ cup (180 mL) whole wheat flour
1 teaspoon (5 mL) active dry yeast
1 teaspoon (5 mL) onion powder
1½ teaspoons (7 mL) vegetable oil

Simple and basic, this chicken is coated with seasoned whole wheat flour and baked until golden. Serve it hot or cold.

1. Heat oven to 400°F (200°C).

2. Dip chicken in water; drain in colander and reserve.

3. Prepare Seasoned Salt. Mix flour, Seasoned Salt, yeast and onion powder in small bowl; drizzle in oil and mix well.

4. Coat chicken evenly on all sides with flour mixture. Arrange chicken in single layer in greased 13x9x2-inch (33x23x5 cm) baking pan.

5. Bake until chicken is tender, 45 to 50 minutes. Serve hot or cold.

Makes about ½ cup (125 mL)

Seasoned Salt

5 tablespoons (75 mL) salt
2 teaspoons (10 mL) celery salt
1 teaspoon (5 mL) garlic powder
1 teaspoon (5 mL) onion powder
1 teaspoon (5 mL) dried sage leaves, crushed
1 teaspoon (5 mL) pepper
½ teaspoon (2 mL) dried oregano leaves, crushed
½ teaspoon (2 mL) paprika
½ teaspoon (2 mL) dried summer savory leaves, crushed
¼ teaspoon (1 mL) vegetable oil

1. Mix all ingredients except oil in small bowl.

2. Drizzle oil over salt mixture; blend well. (All ingredients also can be placed in small blender container and processed on high speed until blended.)

3. Place salt mixture in small tightly covered jar. (Seasoned Salt can be stored covered in refrigerator up to 6 months.)

Floridian Chicken

Spinach Quiche

Chicken Cutlets Celebration

Chicken á la Romanoff

Grecian Kabobs
in Pita Bread

Surprise Potatoes

Crispy Parmesan Chicken

Chicken Cutlets Almondine

Makes 4 servings

2   large whole chicken breasts, deboned, skinned, and split lengthwise into halves
½   teaspoon (2 mL) salt
⅛   teaspoon (0.5 mL) pepper
1   egg, slightly beaten
2   tablespoons (30 mL) milk
⅓   cup (80 mL) sour cream
⅓   cup (80 mL) all-purpose flour
½   cup (125 mL) finely chopped almonds
2   tablespoons (30 mL) butter or margarine
1   tablespoon (15 mL) vegetable oil

These attractive almond-coated boneless chicken breasts go well with buttered asparagus spears, fluffy mashed potatoes and a chilled Chardonnay wine.

1. Flatten chicken by pounding lightly between 2 pieces of waxed paper until ¼ inch (0.5 cm) thick; sprinkle with salt and pepper.

2. Blend egg and 1 tablespoon (15 mL) of the milk in small shallow pan; reserve.

3. Blend sour cream and remaining 1 tablespoon (15 mL) milk in another small shallow pan. Dip each cutlet in sour cream mixture to coat both sides evenly; then dip in flour, pressing to coat both sides evenly. Dip each cutlet in egg mixture, to coat both sides evenly; then dip in almonds, pressing to coat both sides evenly. Place cutlets in single layer on plate; refrigerate until coating sets, about 30 minutes.

4. Heat butter and oil in large skillet over medium heat; add chicken. Cook until chicken is golden, 5 to 7 minutes on each side. Serve hot.

Yogurt-Glazed Chicken

Makes 2 servings

1   cup (250 mL) plain yogurt
1   small onion, cut into quarters
2   tablespoons (30 mL) cider vinegar
2   tablespoons (30 mL) lemon juice
1   clove garlic, cut into halves
1½   teaspoons (7 mL) salt
½   teaspoon (2 mL) ground cumin
½   teaspoon (2 mL) chili powder
¼   teaspoon (1 mL) ground ginger
5   whole coriander seeds or 1 teaspoon (5 mL) ground coriander
1   broiling/frying chicken (about 2 pounds or 900 g), cut into halves

Chicken takes on a unique taste when marinated in yogurt that is blended with exotic Far Eastern spices. This chicken is especially good when grilled and served with watermelon wedges.

1. Measure all ingredients except chicken into blender or food processor container. Cover and blend or process until smooth, about 1 minute.

2. Arrange chicken in shallow baking dish. Cut 2 slashes (each about 2 inches or 5 cm long) with sharp knife through skin on each chicken half.

3. Pour yogurt mixture over chicken. Cover and refrigerate at least 4 hours. Turn chicken over twice during marinating.

4. Heat oven to 375°F (190°C).

5. Remove chicken from marinade and place, skin-side up, in greased shallow baking pan. Brush chicken with marinade.

6. Bake until chicken is tender, about 1 hour. Baste chicken several times during cooking with marinade. Serve hot.

To Cook on Outdoor Grill
Remove chicken from marinade and grill, skin-side up, over slow coals, until golden, 20 to 30 minutes. Turn chicken over. Grill until tender, about 30 minutes longer. Brush chicken frequently with reserved marinade during grilling.

MAIN DISHES

Chicken Cheese Rolls

1 cup (250 mL) Tomato Herb Sauce (see Index for page number)

3 large whole chicken breasts, deboned, skinned and split lengthwise into halves

1 cup (250 mL) small-curd cottage cheese

¼ cup (60 mL) dry bread crumbs

4 tablespoons (60 mL) grated Parmesan cheese

2 tablespoons (30 mL) shredded Monterey Jack or mozzarella cheese

1 tablespoon (15 mL) minced fresh parsley

2 teaspoons (10 mL) instant minced onion

½ teaspoon (2 mL) dried basil leaves

½ teaspoon (2 mL) dried oregano leaves

⅛ teaspoon (0.5 mL) garlic powder

½ cup (125 mL) all-purpose flour

¼ cup (60 mL) butter

¼ cup (60 mL) chicken broth

1½ to 2 pounds (675 to 900 g) zucchini, cut into ¼-inch (0.5 cm) slices

6 thin slices Monterey Jack or mozzarella cheese (about 1 ounce or 30 g each), cut crosswise into halves

Hot cooked white or brown rice

These boneless chicken breasts are filled with a trio of cheeses and baked with fresh zucchini in a rich tomato sauce. They are good served with hot white or brown rice and a bottle of chilled rosé wine.

1. Prepare Tomato Herb Sauce.

2. Heat oven to 350°F (180°C).

3. Flatten chicken by pounding lightly between 2 pieces of waxed paper until ¼ inch (0.5 cm) thick.

4. Mix cottage cheese, bread crumbs, 2 tablespoons (30 mL) of the Parmesan cheese, the shredded Monterey Jack cheese, parsley, onion, basil, oregano and garlic powder in small bowl.

5. Spread about ¼ cup (60 mL) of the cheese mixture lengthwise over center half of each of the 6 chicken pieces; roll each chicken piece around cheese mixture. Press ends firmly together. Dip each roll in flour to coat all sides evenly; reserve.

6. Melt butter in large skillet over medium heat; add chicken. Cook until chicken is golden, 4 to 5 minutes on each side.

7. Blend Tomato Herb Sauce and broth in small bowl. Pour half of the tomato mixture onto a large oven-proof platter or into 13x9x2-inch (33x23x5 cm) baking dish. Place chicken in center of platter; arrange zucchini around chicken. Pour remaining sauce over chicken and zucchini. Sprinkle remaining 2 tablespoons (30 mL) Parmesan cheese over zucchini.

8. Bake until chicken is almost done, about 25 minutes. Arrange cheese slices over chicken; bake until chicken is done, about 10 minutes longer. Serve hot with rice.

Chicken Cutlets Flambé

Makes 4 servings

2   large whole chicken breasts, deboned, skinned and split lengthwise into halves
½   teaspoon (2 mL) salt
⅛   teaspoon (0.5 mL) pepper
¼   cup (60 mL) butter or margarine
8   ounces (225 g) fresh mushrooms, thinly sliced
2   tablespoons (60 mL) thinly sliced green onions
2   tablespoons (60 mL) cognac or brandy
⅓   cup (80 mL) whipping cream
    Watercress, if desired

Easy to prepare, this impressive dish is ideal for entertaining. It consists of boneless chicken breasts and fresh mushrooms that are sautéed in butter and set aflame with cognac before serving in a delicate cream sauce.

1. Flatten chicken by pounding lightly between 2 pieces of waxed paper; sprinkle with salt and pepper.

2. Melt butter in large skillet over medium heat; add chicken. Cook until chicken is golden, 3 to 4 minutes. Turn chicken over; add mushrooms and onion. Cook until mushrooms are tender, 3 to 4 minutes longer.

3. Pour cognac over all; carefully ignite cognac using long wooden match.

4. When flame burns out, stir cream into chicken mixture; cook just until hot, 1 to 2 minutes longer. Serve hot, garnished with watercress.

Bavarian Chicken

Makes 4 servings

8   chicken thighs, deboned and skinned
½   teaspoon (2 mL) salt
⅛   teaspoon (0.5 mL) pepper
2   tablespoons (30 mL) butter or margarine
2   tablespoons (30 ml) vegetable oil
½   cup (125 mL) dry white wine
¼   cup (60 mL) chicken broth
2   tablespoons (30 mL) finely chopped fresh chives
1   teaspoon (5 mL) dried parsley flakes
1   teaspoon (5 mL) all-purpose flour
1   tablespoon (15 mL) water
½   cup (125 mL) sour cream

In this recipe chicken thighs are gently simmered in a wine sauce before sour cream is added. Perfect accompaniments to this hearty main dish would be boiled red cabbage wedges and hot buttered noodles.

1. Sprinkle chicken with salt and pepper.

2. Heat butter and oil in large skillet over medium heat; add chicken. Cook until chicken is golden, 4 to 5 minutes on each side.

3. Add wine, broth, chives and parsley to chicken; heat to boiling. Reduce heat; cover and cook until chicken is done, about 30 minutes. Remove chicken from skillet and place on serving plate; keep warm in 200°F (90°C) oven, if desired.

4. Blend flour and water; stir into broth mixture in skillet. Cook over medium heat, stirring constantly, until thick, about 5 minutes. Stir sour cream into broth mixture; cook just until hot, but not bubbly. Remove from heat. Pour sour cream mixture over chicken; serve hot.

MAIN DISHES

Walnut Chicken

Makes 4 to 6 servings

3   large whole chicken breasts,
    deboned, skinned and
    split lengthwise into
    halves
1½ tablespoons (22 mL)
    cornstarch
2   tablespoons (30 mL) port
    wine
1½ cups (375 mL) chicken
    broth
¼   cup (60 mL) soy sauce
3   tablespoons (45 mL)
    vegetable oil
1½ teaspoons (7 mL) sugar
1   can (5 ounces or 140 g)
    whole bamboo shoots,
    drained and cut into
    halves
¼   cup (60 mL) chopped onion
1   clove garlic, pressed
1   teaspoon (5 mL) freshly
    grated ginger root or ¼
    teaspoon (1 mL) ground
    ginger
1   cup (250 mL) walnut
    halves
    Hot cooked rice

Those who enjoy an Oriental flavor in food will like this dish. Cubes of chicken are stir-fried with walnuts, bamboo shoots, fresh ginger root and soy sauce in this easy entrée that can be cooked in a wok or skillet.

1. Cut chicken into ¼-inch (0.5 cm) cubes; place in small bowl. Add cornstarch and wine to chicken; mix until chicken is coated.

2. Combine ½ cup (125 mL) of the broth, the soy sauce, 2 tablespoons (30 mL) of the oil, and the sugar in wok or large skillet; cook over medium-high heat until hot, 2 to 3 minutes.

3. Add chicken to broth mixture; cook, stirring constantly, until chicken is tender, 3 to 4 minutes longer.

4. Add remaining 1 cup (250 mL) broth; cook until thick, 1 to 2 minutes longer. Remove chicken and thickened broth mixture from wok. Reserve.

5. Add remaining 1 tablespoon (15 mL) of the oil to wok; heat over medium-high heat 1 minute. Add bamboo shoots, onion, garlic and ginger to oil; cook, stirring constantly, until onion is soft, 1 to 2 minutes.

6. Stir walnut halves into bamboo mixture. Return chicken and thickened broth mixture to wok; cook, stirring constantly, until hot. Serve hot over rice.

Floridian Chicken

Makes 4 servings

8   chicken thighs, deboned
    and skinned
½   teaspoon (2 mL) salt
⅛   teaspoon (0.5 mL) pepper
1   tablespoon (15 mL) butter
    or margarine
1   tablespoon (15 mL)
    vegetable oil
3   large carrots, cut diagonally
    into ⅛-inch (0.5 cm)
    slices
1½ cups (375 mL) thinly
    sliced celery
    continued

Grapefruit sections are an interesting addition to this chicken dish that is gently simmered in a tarragon scented sauce.

1. Sprinkle chicken with salt and pepper.

2. Heat butter and oil in large skillet over medium heat; add chicken. Cook until chicken is golden, 4 to 5 minutes on each side.

3. Add carrots, celery, onion, broth, grapefruit juice, sherry and tarragon to chicken; heat to boiling. Reduce heat; cover and cook until chicken is tender, 30 to 40 minutes.

4. Place chicken in center of serving platter. Arrange vegetables around chicken. Keep warm.

92

Floridian Chicken (continued)

1 medium onion, thinly
   sliced
1 cup (250 mL) chicken broth
½ cup (125 mL) grapefruit
   juice
¼ cup (60 mL) dry sherry
1 teaspoon (5 mL) dried
   tarragon leaves
2 tablespoons (30 mL) water
1½ teaspoons (7 mL)
   cornstarch
1 grapefruit, peeled and
   sectioned
   Fresh mint leaves, if
   desired

5. Blend water and cornstarch in small bowl; stir into sauce in skillet. Cook, stirring constantly, until thick about 2 minutes.

6. Add grapefruit to cornstarch mixture; cook until grapefruit is hot. Pour the sauce over chicken and vegetables. Garnish with mint leaves.

Makes 4 servings

Breast of Chicken Madeira

½ package (17¼-ounce or
   489 g size) frozen puff
   pastry (1 sheet, about
   9½ inches or 24.5 cm
   square)
   All-purpose flour
2 large whole chicken breasts,
   deboned, skinned and
   split lengthwise into
   halves
¼ teaspoon (1 mL) salt
⅛ teaspoon (0.5 mL) pepper
¼ cup (60 mL) butter or
   margarine
1 egg, slightly beaten
   Madeira Sauce (see Index
   for page number)

This elegant entrée is perfect for entertaining. Sautéed boneless chicken breasts are encased in crisp, flaky puff pastry and served with an easy but sophisticated Madeira wine sauce.

1. Thaw pastry at room temperature 20 minutes. Unfold pastry sheet; cut sheet into 4 squares (4¾ inches or 12 cm each). Roll each square on lightly floured surface into a 6½-inch (16.5 cm) square. Reserve.

2. Heat oven to 350°F (180°C).

3. Sprinkle chicken with salt and pepper.

4. Melt butter in large skillet over medium heat; add chicken. Cook until chicken is light brown, about 2 minutes on each side. Remove chicken from pan; reserve.

5. Place 1 piece chicken over lower half of 1 pastry square; fold top half of pastry over chicken; pinch edges well to seal in chicken. Repeat procedure with remaining chicken and dough.

6. Place filled pastries on greased cookie sheet; brush evenly with egg. Bake until pastries are golden, about 20 minutes.

7. While pastries are baking, prepare Madeira Sauce.

8. Place pastries on serving plates; pour a scant ⅓ cup (80 mL) Madeira Sauce over each. Serve hot.

MAIN DISHES

Chicken Continental

Makes 4 servings

2   large whole chicken breasts, deboned, skinned and split lengthwise into halves

6   tablespoons (90 mL) butter or margarine

½   teaspoon (2 mL) salt

¼   teaspoon (1 mL) ground pepper

3   ounces (85 g) sliced cooked ham, cut into ¼-inch (0.5 cm) wide strips

½   cup (125 mL) finely chopped green pepper

8   ounces (225 mL) fresh mushrooms, sliced

3   cups (750 mL) fresh tomatoes, peeled, seeded and diced (about 1½ pounds or 675 g)

4   slices Vermouth French Toast (see Index for page number) or hot cooked rice

1   cup (250 mL) diced or shredded sharp Cheddar cheese (4 ounces or 115 g)

This combination of chicken, ham, fresh vegetables and cheese can be put together in less than 1 hour. It's delicious served over French toast or hot cooked rice accompanied by a crisp leafy green salad.

1. Cut chicken into 2x¼-inch (5x0.5 cm) strips.

2. Melt butter in large skillet over medium heat; add chicken. Sprinkle chicken with salt and pepper. Cook until chicken is golden, 3 to 4 minutes.

3. Add ham, green pepper and mushrooms to chicken; cook 2 to 3 minutes longer.

4. Add tomatoes to chicken mixture; cook 5 minutes longer. Reduce heat; cover and cook 15 to 20 minutes longer.

5. Meanwhile, prepare Vermouth French Toast or rice.

6. Uncover skillet, add cheese and cook, stirring occasionally, until cheese melts, 3 to 5 minutes longer. Serve hot over Vermouth French Toast or rice.

Tarragon Chicken

Makes 4 servings

1   broiling/frying chicken (about 3 pounds or 1350 g), cut into serving pieces

1½   teaspoons (7 mL) salt

¼   teaspoon (1 mL) pepper

3   tablespoons (45 mL) butter or margarine

1   tablespoon (15 mL) vegetable oil

1   tablespoon (15 mL) minced fresh parsley

continued

In this easy main dish, chicken pieces are sautéed and then simmered in a fresh tarragon-wine sauce for an enticing entrée. Complete the menu by adding a tossed green salad, fluffy white rice and hot buttered French bread.

1. Sprinkle chicken with salt and pepper.

2. Heat butter and oil in large skillet over medium heat until butter melts; add parsley, 1 tablespoon (15 mL) of the fresh or 1 teaspoon (5 mL) of the dried tarragon and the garlic. Place chicken, skin-side down, in butter mixture. Cook until chicken is golden, 7 to 8 minutes.

3. Turn chicken over, cook until chicken is golden, 7 to 8 minutes longer. Remove chicken from skillet; reserve.

Tarragon Chicken (continued)

---

2 tablespoons (30 mL) chopped fresh or 2 teaspoons (10 mL) dried tarragon leaves

1 clove garlic, pressed

⅓ cup (80 mL) chopped onion

½ cup (125 mL) dry white wine

3 tablespoons (45 mL) all-purpose flour

1 cup (250 mL) milk

4. Add onion to drippings in skillet; cook until onion is golden, about 3 minutes. Stir in wine and remaining 1 tablespoon (15 mL) fresh or 1 teaspoon (5 mL) dried tarragon; add chicken. Spoon wine mixture over chicken; cover and cook until chicken is almost done, about 20 minutes. Remove chicken from skillet.

5. Mix flour with ¼ cup (60 mL) of the milk in small bowl. Blend flour mixture and remaining ¾ cup (180 mL) milk into tarragon sauce. Cook, stirring frequently, until sauce is thick, 2 to 3 minutes. Return chicken to skillet. Reduce heat; cook until chicken is tender, 8 to 10 minutes longer. Serve hot.

Makes 4 servings

Pollo al Romano

3 whole chicken breasts (about 10 ounces or 285 g each) deboned, skinned and split lengthwise into halves

1 teaspoon (5 mL) lemon juice

½ teaspoon (2 mL) dried Italian herbs

¼ teaspoon (1 mL) salt

⅛ teaspoon (0.5 mL) pepper

¼ cup (60 mL) butter or margarine

1 small onion, chopped

1 small clove garlic, minced

1 tomato, peeled and chopped

1 cup (250 mL) chicken broth

⅓ cup (80 mL) cubed Romano cheese (about 3 ounces or 85 g)

1 package (8 ounces or 225 g) medium-wide egg noodles, cooked and drained

Easy to prepare in a hurry, this Italian-style dish consists of boneless chicken strips that are seasoned with Italian herbs and topped with Romano cheese. The entrée is delicious served with homemade noodles and a seasonal fresh fruit salad.

1. Cut chicken into 2x¼-inch (5x0.5 cm) strips; sprinkle with lemon juice, herbs, salt and pepper.

2. Melt butter in large skillet over medium heat; add chicken, onion and garlic. Cook, stirring frequently, until chicken is golden, 5 to 7 minutes.

3. Add tomato and broth to chicken. Reduce heat; cover and cook 10 minutes longer.

4. Add cheese to chicken mixture; cover and cook until cheese melts, about 3 minutes longer. Serve hot over noodles.

MAIN DISHES

Chicken Kiev

Makes 4 to 6 servings

6 tablespoons (90 mL) cold butter
1½ tablespoons (22 mL) minced fresh parsley
1½ tablespoons (22 mL) minced fresh chives
1 teaspoon (5 mL) dried tarragon leaves
½ teaspoon (2 mL) dried oregano leaves
½ teaspoon (2 mL) dried thyme leaves
Vegetable oil
3 large whole chicken breasts, deboned, skinned and split lengthwise into halves
¼ cup (60 mL) all-purpose flour
1 egg, beaten
½ cup (125 mL) dry bread crumbs

This classic recipe, named after the Ukranian city of Kiev, consists of boneless chicken breasts that are wrapped around herb-seasoned butter, then breaded and deep-fried.

1. Cut butter into 6 pieces; shape each into a roll about ½-inch (1.5 cm) thick.

2. Mix parsley, chives, tarragon, oregano and thyme in small bowl. Roll butter in herbs to coat evenly; freeze butter about 30 minutes.

3. Pour oil into deep fryer or 5-quart (5 L) Dutch oven until it reaches a level 2½ to 3 inches (6.5 to 8 cm) deep. Heat to 350°F (180°C).

4. Flatten chicken by pounding lightly between 2 pieces of waxed paper until ¼ inch (0.5 cm) thick.

5. Place 1 frozen butter roll in center of 1 flattened chicken piece; carefully fold chicken completely around butter. Secure with wooden pick. Repeat with remaining chicken and butter.

6. Roll each chicken piece in flour to coat completely; then dip in egg and roll in bread crumbs to coat completely.

7. Fry chicken in oil until golden, about 5 minutes. Drain on paper toweling. Serve immediately.

Chicken Roulades

Makes 4 servings

2 large whole chicken breasts, deboned, skinned and split lengthwise into halves
6 small bratwurst or Italian sausages
2 tablespoons (30 mL) finely chopped celery leaves
¼ teaspoon (1 mL) salt
⅛ teaspoon (0.5 mL) ground sage
⅛ teaspoon (0.5 mL) pepper
2 tablespoons (30 mL) butter or margarine
¼ cup (60 mL) Madeira wine

Boneless chicken breasts are wrapped around a hearty sausage filling in this version of the popular German dish. Braised sauerkraut, hot German potato salad and rye bread would be good choices for serving with this dish.

1. Flatten chicken by pounding lightly between 2 pieces of waxed paper until ¼ inch (0.5 cm) thick.

2. Remove and discard skins from bratwurst. Place bratwurst in small skillet and break into small pieces using fork. Cook over medium heat, stirring frequently, until bratwurst is golden, about 10 minutes.

3. Add celery leaves, salt, sage and pepper to bratwurst; cook, stirring constantly, 1 minute longer. Remove from heat.

4. Arrange ¼ of the bratwurst mixture over 1 cutlet, leaving ½ inch (1.5 cm) uncovered at edges. Roll cutlet up jelly-roll fashion; press ends together firmly. Repeat procedure to shape remaining cutlets.

5. Heat oven to 350°F (180°C). *continued*

Chicken Roulades (continued)

6. Melt butter in large skillet over medium heat; add chicken rolls, seam-side down. Cook until chicken is golden, 4 to 5 minutes on each side.

7. Place chicken in 11x7x2-inch (28x18x5 cm) baking dish; pour wine and pan drippings over chicken. Cover tightly.

8. Bake until chicken is done, about 30 minutes. Serve hot.

Chicken à la Romanoff

Makes 4 servings

3 cups (750 mL) water
1¾ teaspoons (9 mL) salt
2 tablespoons (30 mL) plus ½ teaspoon (2 mL) vegetable oil
½ cup (125 mL) uncooked fine egg noodles (about 1 ounce or 30 g)
2 large whole chicken breasts, deboned, skinned and split lengthwise into halves
¼ teaspoon (1 mL) plus ⅛ teaspoon (0.5 mL) white pepper
1½ ounces (45 g) cream cheese, at room temperature
¼ cup (60 mL) sour cream
1 tablespoon (15 mL) grated Parmesan cheese
1 teaspoon (5 mL) minced fresh chives
⅛ teaspoon (0.5 mL) garlic powder
1 egg
¼ cup (60 mL) milk
½ cup (125 mL) whole wheat or all-purpose flour
¼ cup (60 mL) butter or margarine
Champignon Sauce (see Index for page number)

Elegant for entertaining, this entrée features boneless chicken breasts wrapped around a delicate mixture of cream cheese, noodles and sour cream. The breasts are sautéed until golden and served with a lucious mushroom sauce.

1. Heat water in 2-quart (2 L) saucepan over high heat to boiling; add ½ teaspoon (2 mL) of the salt and ½ teaspoon (2 mL) oil. Gradually stir noodles into water. Cook until noodles are tender but firm, about 5 minutes. Drain noodles and rinse with cold water; drain again.

2. Flatten chicken by pounding lightly between 2 pieces of waxed paper until ¼-inch (0.5 cm) thick; sprinkle or rub with 1 teaspoon (5 mL) of the remaining salt and ¼ teaspoon (1 mL) pepper.

3. Mix cream cheese, sour cream, Parmesan cheese, chives, remaining ¼ teaspoon (1 mL) salt, remaining ⅛ teaspoon (0.5 mL) pepper and the garlic powder in medium bowl. Add noodles to cheese mixture; mix well.

4. Spread ¼ of the noodle mixture over center of each chicken piece; fold sides of chicken over to cover filling. Secure with wooden picks. Refrigerate chicken 15 minutes.

5. Beat egg and milk in shallow pan. Dip chicken in egg mixture to coat all sides evenly; then dip in flour to coat all sides evenly. Refrigerate chicken 30 minutes.

6. Heat oven to 375°F (190°C).

7. Heat butter and remaining 2 tablespoons (30 mL) oil in medium skillet over medium heat; add chicken. Cook until chicken is golden, 4 to 5 minutes on each side. Remove chicken from skillet, reserve.

8. Brush pan drippings evenly over bottom of 9-inch (23 cm) square baking dish; add chicken. Bake until chicken is tender, 20 to 25 minutes.

9. Prepare Champignon Sauce.

10. Arrange chicken on serving plate; spoon about 1 cup (250 mL) of the Champignon Sauce over chicken. Pass remaining sauce. Serve hot.

MAIN DISHES

Almond Pilaff

Makes 4 servings

5   cups (1250 mL) water
2   cups (500 mL) uncooked
       rice
2   teaspoons (10 mL) salt
½   teaspoon (2 mL) sugar
1   teaspoon (5 mL) lemon
       juice
8   tablespoons (125 mL)
       butter or margarine
2   large whole chicken breasts,
       deboned, skinned and
       split lengthwise into
       halves
⅛   teaspoon (0.5 mL) pepper
⅛   teaspoon (0.5 mL) ground
       cinnamon
½   cup (125 mL) blanched
       whole almonds, cut
       lengthwise into halves
       and toasted
       Raisin Sauce (see Index for
       page number)

A golden raisin sauce is the perfect complement to this interesting chicken, rice and almond mold.

1. Heat oven to 350°F (180°C).

2. Heat water in 3-quart (3 L) saucepan over high heat to boiling; stir in rice, 1½ teaspoons (7 mL) of the salt, the sugar, lemon juice and 2 tablespoons (30 mL) of the butter.

3. Reduce heat to low; cover and cook until water is absorbed, about 25 minutes. Remove from heat. Add 4 tablespoons (60 mL) of the remaining butter; stir until butter melts.

4. Flatten chicken by pounding lightly between 2 pieces of waxed paper until ¼-inch (0.5 cm) thick. Cut chicken into 2x1-inch (5x2.5 cm) strips; sprinkle with remaining ½ teaspoon (2 mL) salt, the pepper and cinnamon.

5. Melt remaining 2 tablespoons (30 mL) butter in large skillet over medium heat; add chicken. Cook until chicken is golden, 3 to 4 minutes on each side. Remove from skillet; reserve.

6. Line bottom of well greased 8-cup (2 L) mold with almonds. Arrange chicken pieces around edges of mold. Pack rice firmly into mold. Cover mold with aluminum foil; place a plate on top of foil and press down firmly over rice. Bake 15 minutes.

7. While pilaff is baking, prepare Raisin Sauce.

8. Remove plate and aluminum foil from mold; place serving dish over mold. Invert and unmold. Pour Raisin Sauce over pilaff; serve immediately.

Sophie's Party Chicken

Makes 8 servings

2   teaspoons (10 mL) Seasoned
       Salt (see Index for page
       number)
4   large whole chicken breasts,
       deboned, skinned and
       split lengthwise into
       halves
1   package (17¼ ounces or
       489 g) frozen puff pastry
       (2 sheets, each about
       9½ inches or 24.5 cm
       square)
       continued

This entrée is well worth the bit of extra effort it may take to prepare. Sautéed boneless chicken breasts are tucked between two layers of flaky puff pastry and served with an elegant sauce.

1. Prepare Seasoned Salt.

2. Flatten chicken by pounding lightly between 2 pieces of waxed paper until ¼ inch (0.5 cm) thick; rub with Seasoned Salt. Place chicken in shallow glass dish; cover and refrigerate about 1 hour.

3. Thaw pastry at room temperature 20 minutes. Unfold pastry sheets; cut each sheet into 4 squares (4¾ inches or 12 cm each).

4. Heat oven to 350°F (180°C).

Sophie's Party Chicken *(continued)*

1   egg, slightly beaten
     Bordelaise Sauce (see Index
        for page number)
¼   cup (60 mL) butter or
        margarine
1   tablespoon (15 mL)
        vegetable oil

5. Place pastry squares on greased cookie sheets; brush evenly with egg. Bake until pastries are golden, about 20 minutes.

6. While pastries are baking, prepare Bordelaise Sauce. Keep warm.

7. Cool pastries completely on wire rack. Carefully cut each pastry in half horizontally with sharp knife; reserve.

8. Heat butter and oil in large skillet over medium heat; add half of the chicken. Cook until chicken is golden, about 4 minutes on each side. Remove chicken from skillet; keep warm. Repeat procedure to cook remaining chicken.

9. Return all chicken to skillet. Reduce heat; cover and cook until chicken is tender, about 5 minutes longer.

10. Place 1 chicken piece on 1 pastry half; spread with 1 tablespoon (15 mL) of the Bordelaise Sauce. Cover chicken with other half of pastry. Repeat with remaining pastries and chicken; place on serving platter. Serve immediately with remaining sauce.

Makes 4 to 6 servings

Crepes Ratatouille

12   Crepes (see Index for page
         number)
      Swiss Cheese Sauce (see
         Index for page number)
¼   cup (60 mL) butter or
         margarine
2   cups (500 mL) diced
         cooked chicken
2   cups (500 mL) diced
         zucchini (about 2
         medium zucchini)
½   package (10-ounce or
         285 g size) frozen cut
         green beans
1   large stalk celery, cut
         diagonally into ¼-inch
         (0.5 cm) slices
½   cup (125 mL) diced carrot
2   green onions, thinly sliced

In this lovely entrée, lacy crepes are wrapped around a savory chicken and vegetable filling before baking with a velvety Swiss cheese sauce.

1. Prepare Crepes.

2. Prepare Swiss Cheese Sauce.

3. Heat oven to 375°F (190°C).

4. Melt butter in large skillet over medium heat; remove and reserve 1 tablespoon (15 mL) of the melted butter. Add chicken, zucchini, beans, celery, carrot and onion to remaining butter in skillet. Cook, stirring occasionally, until vegetables are crisp-tender, about 5 minutes. Remove chicken mixture from heat.

5. Stir 1 cup (250 mL) of the Swiss Cheese Sauce into the chicken mixture; mix to coat all ingredients. Reserve remaining ½ cup (125 mL) sauce.

6. Spoon about ⅓ cup (80 mL) of the chicken mixture evenly across center of each crepe. Fold over one side of each crepe, covering most of filling. Fold over opposite side, overlapping first fold. Repeat until all crepes are folded.

7. Place crepes, folded edge up, in greased 13x9x2-inch (33x23x5 cm) baking pan. Brush tops of crepes with reserved 1 tablespoon (15 mL) melted butter. Pour remaining cheese sauce over crepes.

8. Bake until crepes are hot throughout, about 15 minutes. Serve hot.

MAIN DISHES

Banana-Chick Broil

Makes 6 servings

4 large whole chicken breasts, deboned, skinned and split lengthwise into halves
2 tablespoons (30 mL) soy sauce
2 tablespoons (30 mL) vegetable oil
2 tablespoons (30 mL) lemon juice
⅛ teaspoon (0.5 mL) garlic powder
⅛ teaspoon (0.5 mL) pepper
3 large firm bananas
1 tablespoon (15 mL) butter or margarine, at room temperature
1 tablespoon (15 mL) brown sugar

Boneless chicken breasts are marinated in a flavorful soy sauce before broiling. During the last few minutes of broiling, buttered and sugared banana slices are added.

1. Place chicken in 1½-quart (1.5 L) rectangular baking dish.

2. Mix soy sauce, oil, lemon juice, garlic powder and pepper in small bowl; pour over chicken. Cover and refrigerate 3 to 4 hours; turn chicken over 2 or 3 times during marinating.

3. Remove chicken from marinade and arrange on greased broiler pan. Broil 6 inches (15 cm) from heat until chicken is golden, 5 to 6 minutes. Brush chicken with marinade and turn chicken over; broil 2 minutes longer.

4. Remove chicken from broiler. Peel bananas and cut lengthwise into halves; place bananas on broiler pan with chicken. Brush bananas with butter and sprinkle with sugar. Broil until chicken is done, 2 to 3 minutes longer. Serve hot.

Caribbean Chicken

Makes 4 servings

3 medium carrots, cut into ¼-inch (0.5 cm) slices
2 tablespoons (30 mL) water
¼ cup (60 mL) butter or margarine
2 cups (500 mL) coarsely chopped cooked chicken
1 tablespoon (15 mL) lemon juice
2 teaspoons (10 mL) brown sugar
½ teaspoon (2 mL) salt
½ teaspoon (2 mL) ground coriander
1 large firm banana, cut into ¼-inch (0.5 cm) slices
1 tablespoon (15 mL) chopped fresh parsley, if desired
Hot cooked rice

Crispy carrot and delicate banana slices are added to this chicken dish for a delightfully unique combination of flavors.

1. Place carrots and water in small saucepan; heat to boiling over high heat. Reduce heat to low; cover and cook about 4 minutes. Drain carrots and reserve.

2. Melt butter in large skillet over medium heat; add carrots, chicken, lemon juice, brown sugar, salt and coriander. Cook, stirring constantly, until hot throughout, about 3 minutes.

3. Add banana to chicken mixture; cook and stir until banana is hot, about 2 minutes. Sprinkle with parsley; serve hot with rice.

Saltimbocca

Makes 4 servings

2   large whole chicken breasts, deboned, skinned and split lengthwise into halves

4   slices (each 3½ inches or 9 cm square) boiled ham (about 1 ounce or 30 g each)

¼   cup (60 mL) grated Parmesan cheese

3   tablespoons (45 mL) all-purpose flour

¾   teaspoon (4 mL) salt

½   teaspoon (2 mL) ground sage

¼   teaspoon (1 mL) pepper

¼   cup (60 mL) butter or margarine

3   tablespoons (45 mL) olive or vegetable oil

1   can (10½ ounces or 300 g) condensed chicken broth

In this Italian main dish, boneless chicken breasts are sandwiched with ham slices and dipped in a cheese coating before sautéeing. Convenient for entertaining, the chicken can be completely assembled in advance and held in the refrigerator until ready to cook.

1. Cut chicken pieces crosswise into halves, making 8 pieces. Flatten pieces by pounding lightly between 2 pieces of waxed paper until about ⅛ inch (0.5 cm) thick.

2. Place 1 ham slice between 2 flattened chicken pieces; tie together with thread.

3. Mix cheese, flour, salt, sage and pepper in shallow pan. Dip chicken pieces in cheese mixture, pressing firmly to coat both sides evenly; shake off excess. Reserve ¼ cup (60 mL) of the remaining cheese mixture. Refrigerate chicken 30 minutes.

4. Heat butter and oil in large skillet over medium heat; add chicken. Cook until chicken is golden, 4 to 5 minutes on each side. Drain on paper toweling.

5. Pour ¼ cup (60 mL) of the pan drippings into small saucepan. Stir in reserved cheese mixture and broth. Cook over low heat, stirring constantly, until sauce is thick, about 5 minutes. Pour sauce over chicken. Serve hot.

Sherried Chicken with Zucchini

Makes 2 servings

4   chicken thighs, deboned and skinned

¾   cup (180 mL) French dressing

2   tablespoons (30 mL) dry sherry

    Pinch garlic salt

3   tablespoons (45 mL) butter

1   tablespoon (15 mL) vegetable oil

1   pound (450 g) zucchini, cut lengthwise into ⅜-inch (1 cm) thick slices

This is a simple yet flavorful main dish. The boneless chicken and sliced zucchini are laced with sherry and French dressing.

1. Place chicken in shallow dish or pie plate.

2. Blend French dressing, sherry and garlic salt in small bowl; pour over chicken. Turn chicken to coat both sides. Cover and refrigerate 1 hour.

3. Heat butter and oil in large skillet over medium heat. Remove chicken from marinade; drain chicken, reserving marinade. Cook chicken in the butter mixture until golden, 4 to 5 minutes on each side. Cover and cook until chicken is tender, about 20 minutes. Remove chicken from skillet; keep warm.

4. Dip zucchini into remaining marinade, turning to coat both sides. Cook in pan drippings until zucchini are golden, about 2 minutes on each side. Arrange chicken and zucchini on serving plate. Serve hot.

Fried Chicken

If you like your chicken fried, you'll love
the recipes in this chapter. From Honey "Dipt" Chicken
to Batter Fried Chicken,
it includes all varieties: pan-fried, deep-fried
and oven-fried.

Honey "Dipt" Chicken

Makes 4 servings

Spiced Fruit (recipe follows)
1   broiling/frying chicken
    (about 3 pounds or
    1350 g), cut into serving
    pieces
½   cup (125 mL) water
1   teaspoon (5 mL) salt
¼   teaspoon (1 mL) pepper
½   cup (125 mL) all-purpose
    flour
3   tablespoons (45 mL)
    vegetable oil
2   tablespoons (30 mL) butter
    or margarine
¾   cup (180 mL) honey

*This easy chicken is fried in a skillet until it is crisp and golden on the
outside, moist and tender on the inside. Just before serving, it is dipped in
honey.*

1. Prepare Spiced Fruit.

2. Dip chicken in water; shake off excess water. Sprinkle chicken with salt
and pepper. Coat chicken evenly on all sides with flour. Place chicken on
wire rack and let dry 15 minutes.

3. Heat oil and butter in large skillet over medium heat; add chicken,
skin-side down. Cook 20 to 25 minutes. Turn chicken over; cook until
chicken is tender, about 30 minutes longer.

4. Remove chicken from skillet; drain on paper toweling. Dip chicken
immediately in honey to coat all sides. Serve hot, garnished with Spiced
Fruit.

Spiced Fruit

Makes 8 servings

1   can (29 ounces or 820 g)
    peach, pear or apricot
    halves
2   tablespoons (30 mL) port
    wine
2   tablespoons (30 mL) cider
    vinegar
½   teaspoon (2 mL) whole
    cloves
1   stick cinnamon (about
    2 inches or 5 cm long)

1. Drain fruit, reserving juice. Place juice, wine, vinegar, cloves and
cinnamon stick in 1-quart (1 L) saucepan. Cook over high heat until
mixture boils. Reduce heat to low; simmer 10 minutes.

2. Add fruit to juice mixture. Simmer 5 minutes longer. Remove from
heat; pour into container with cover. Refrigerate several hours or
overnight to blend flavors. (Fruit will keep covered in refrigerator up to
1 week.)

Deep-Fried Chicken

Makes 4 servings

1 broiling/frying chicken (about 3 pounds or 1350 g), cut into serving pieces
1 stalk celery (including leaves), cut into 2-inch (5 cm) pieces
1 small onion, cut into halves
1 clove garlic, cut into halves
2½ teaspoons (12 mL) salt
1 teaspoon (5 mL) pepper
1¾ cups (430 mL) water
½ cup (125 mL) all-purpose flour
½ teaspoon (2 mL) garlic powder
Vegetable oil

A crisp, golden coating seals in all the juicy flavor in this traditional fried chicken. Allowing the coating to dry and set before deep-frying makes the chicken crisper.

1. Place chicken, celery, onion, garlic, ½ teaspoon (2 mL) of the salt, ¼ teaspoon (1 mL) of the pepper and 1 cup (250 mL) of the water in 5-quart (5 L) Dutch oven; heat to boiling over high heat. Reduce heat to low; cover and cook until chicken is almost tender, about 30 minutes.

2. Remove chicken from Dutch oven, drain and pat dry with paper toweling. Cool slightly.

3. Combine flour, remaining 2 teaspoons (10 mL) salt, ¾ teaspoon (4 mL) pepper and the garlic powder in shallow pan. Dip chicken in remaining ¾ cup (180 mL) water, then dip in flour mixture, pressing to coat all sides evenly. Place chicken on wire rack and let dry 15 minutes.

4. Pour oil into deep fryer or 5-quart (5 L) Dutch oven until it reaches a level 2½ to 3 inches (6.5 to 8 cm) deep. Heat oil to 350°F (180°C).

5. Add several chicken pieces to oil. (Do not crowd; pieces should not touch each other.) Fry, turning occasionally, until chicken browns evenly on all sides, 10 to 12 minutes.

6. Place fried chicken on cookie sheet lined with paper toweling; keep warm in 200°F (90°C) oven until ready to serve.

Lemon Chicken

Makes 4 servings

1 broiling/frying chicken (about 3 pounds or 1350 g), cut into serving pieces
2 tablespoons (30 mL) butter or margarine, at room temperature
2 tablespoons (30 mL) olive or vegetable oil
2 tablespoons (30 mL) lemon juice
1 teaspoon (5 mL) salt
1 teaspoon (5 mL) dried oregano leaves
¼ teaspoon (1 mL) pepper
4 medium potatoes, cut lengthwise into quarters

For economy and convenience, chicken and potatoes are oven-fried together and basted with the pan juices.

1. Heat oven to 400°F (200°C).

2. Brush chicken with butter. Beat oil, lemon juice, salt, oregano and pepper in small bowl with fork. Brush chicken on all sides with oil mixture.

3. Arrange chicken, skin-side down, in single layer in 15½x10½x1-inch (39x26.5x2.5 cm) jelly-roll pan. (Pieces should not touch.) Bake 15 minutes. Baste with pan juices; bake 15 minutes longer. Turn chicken over. Arrange potatoes with chicken in pan; baste with pan juices. Bake until chicken and potatoes are golden and tender, 25 to 30 minutes longer.

4. Arrange chicken and potatoes on serving platter; pour pan drippings over all. Serve hot.

FRIED CHICKEN

Oven-Fried Chicken

Makes 4 servings

Seasoned Bread Crumbs
(recipe follows)
1   broiling/frying chicken
    (about 3 pounds or
    1350 g), cut into serving
    pieces
½   cup (125 mL) evaporated
    milk
3   tablespoons (45 mL)
    vegetable oil

*For an old-fashioned meal, serve this crisp, herb-seasoned chicken with
hot biscuits and corn-on-the-cob. Kabobs made of fresh fruit in season
make a nice finishing touch.*

1. Prepare Seasoned Bread Crumbs.

2. Heat oven to 375°F (190°C).

3. Dip chicken in bread crumbs, then in milk; dip again in crumbs,
pressing to coat all sides evenly. Arrange chicken, skin-side up, on greased
15½x10½x1-inch (39x26.5x2.5 cm) jelly-roll pan. (Pieces should not
touch.)

4. Bake 30 minutes. Drizzle chicken with oil. Bake until chicken is golden
and crisp about 30 minutes longer. Serve hot or cold.

Seasoned Bread Crumbs

Makes about 1 cup (250 mL)

1   cup (250 mL) fine dry
    bread crumbs
2   teaspoons (10 mL) salt
2   teaspoons (10 mL) dried
    summer savory leaves,
    crushed
2   teaspoons (10 mL) dried
    thyme leaves, crushed
2   teaspoons (10 mL) paprika
1   teaspoon (5 mL) dried
    marjoram leaves, crushed
1   teaspoon (5 mL) lemon
    pepper
½   teaspoon (2 mL) celery salt
½   teaspoon (2 mL) onion
    powder
½   teaspoon (2 mL) ground
    mace
¼   teaspoon (1 mL) garlic
    powder

1. Mix all ingredients in bowl. (Mixture can be stored in tightly covered
container in refrigerator up to 2 months.)

Crispy Parmesan Chicken

Makes 4 servings

¾ cup (180 mL) crushed
    saltine crackers, corn
    flakes or potato chips
⅓ cup (80 mL) grated
    Parmesan cheese
¾ teaspoon (4 mL) salt
½ teaspoon (2 mL) celery salt
½ teaspoon (2 mL) paprika
¼ teaspoon (1 mL) onion
    powder
¼ teaspoon (1 mL) pepper
3 tablespoons (45 mL)
    evaporated milk
3 tablespoons (45 mL)
    vegetable oil
1 broiling/frying chicken
    (about 3 pounds or
    1350 g), cut into serving
    pieces

You'll want to keep this recipe for a simple oven-fried chicken handy for frequent use.

1. Heat oven to 375°F (190°C).

2. Mix crushed crackers, cheese, salt, celery salt, paprika, onion powder and pepper in shallow pan.

3. Blend milk and oil in another small shallow pan. Dip chicken in milk mixture, then in crumb mixture, pressing to coat all sides evenly.

4. Arrange chicken, skin-side up, in shallow baking pan. Bake until chicken is tender, about 1 hour. Serve hot or cold.

Pecan Chicken

Makes 4 servings

1 cup (250 mL) biscuit
    baking mix
½ cup (125 mL) finely
    chopped pecans
2 teaspoons (10 mL) paprika
1 teaspoon (5 mL) salt
½ teaspoon (2 mL) dried sage
    leaves
½ teaspoon (2 mL) dried
    tarragon leaves
⅓ cup (80 mL) evaporated
    milk
1 broiling/frying chicken
    (about 3 pounds or
    1350 g), cut into serving
    pieces
¼ cup (60 mL) butter or
    margarine, melted

Pecans and herbs combine to add exciting flavor to this crisp, oven-fried chicken.

1. Heat oven to 375°F (190°C).

2. Combine biscuit mix, pecans and seasonings in shallow pan; mix well. Pour milk into another shallow pan. Dip chicken in milk; then dip in pecan mixture, pressing to coat all sides evenly. Repeat, dipping pieces again in milk and then in pecan mixture, pressing to coat all sides evenly.

3. Arrange chicken, skin-side up, in single layer in greased 15½x10½x1-inch (39x26.5x2.5 cm) jelly-roll pan. (Pieces should not touch.) Drizzle butter over chicken. Bake until chicken is tender, about 1 hour. Serve hot.

FRIED CHICKEN

Makes 4 servings

Southern Fried Chicken with Cream Gravy

1   broiling/frying chicken (about 3 pounds or 1350 g), cut into serving pieces
½   cup (125 mL) water or milk
2   teaspoons (10 mL) salt
½   teaspoon (2 mL) pepper
½   cup (125 mL) plus 3 tablespoons (45 mL) all-purpose flour
2   cups (500 mL) half and half
    Vegetable oil

This wonderful skillet-fried chicken is served with a deliciously rich cream gravy.

1. Dip chicken in water; shake off excess water. Sprinkle chicken with salt and pepper.

2. Coat chicken evenly on all sides with ½ cup (125 mL) of the flour. Place chicken on wire rack and let dry 15 minutes.

3. Pour enough oil in large, deep skillet to reach a level ½ inch (1.5 cm) deep. Heat over medium heat until hot enough to sizzle a drop of water; add chicken, skin-side down. Cook 10 minutes. Reduce heat to low; cook 20 minutes longer.

4. Turn chicken pieces over. Cook until chicken is tender, 15 to 20 minutes longer.

5. Remove chicken pieces from pan, reserving drippings. Drain chicken on paper toweling; keep warm in 200°F (90°C) oven while preparing gravy.

6. Scrape browned bits from bottom of pan. Place browned bits and ¼ cup (60 mL) of pan drippings in small saucepan; blend in remaining 3 tablespoons (45 mL) flour. Cook over medium heat, stirring constantly, until bubbly, 1 to 2 minutes. Stir half and half into flour mixture; cook, stirring constantly, until gravy is thick, about 5 minutes. Serve chicken hot with gravy.

Makes 4 servings

Batter Fried Chicken

1   broiling/frying chicken (about 3 pounds or 1350 g), cut into serving pieces
1   cup (250 mL) water
1   stalk celery (including leaves), cut into 2-inch (5 cm) pieces
1   small onion, cut into halves
1   clove garlic, cut into halves
½   teaspoon (2 mL) salt
⅛   teaspoon (0.5 mL) pepper
    Fritter Batter (recipe follows)
    Vegetable oil

This unbeatable chicken is steamed until almost tender, then dipped in a delicate fritter batter and deep-fried until golden and crispy.

1. Place chicken, water, celery, onion, garlic, salt and pepper in 5-quart (5 L) Dutch oven; heat to boiling over high heat. Reduce heat to low; cover and cook until chicken is almost tender, 20 to 25 minutes.

2. While chicken is cooking, prepare Fritter Batter.

3. Remove chicken from Dutch oven, drain and pat dry with paper toweling. Cool slightly.

4. Pour oil into deep fryer or 5-quart (5 L) Dutch oven until it reaches a level 2½ to 3 inches (6.5 to 8 cm) deep. Heat oil to 350°F (180°C).

5. Dip chicken in Fritter Batter to coat all sides evenly. Add several chicken pieces to oil. (Do not crowd; pieces should not touch each other.) Fry, turning occasionally, until chicken is golden, 5 to 7 minutes.

6. Place fried chicken on cookie sheet lined with paper toweling; keep warm in 200°F (90°C) oven until ready to serve.

Makes about 1½ cups (375 mL)

Fritter Batter

1 cup (250 mL) all-purpose
　flour
1 teaspoon (5 mL) baking
　powder
1 teaspoon (5 mL) salt
¼ teaspoon (1 mL) white
　pepper
2 eggs
¾ cup (180 mL) milk
1 tablespoon (15 mL)
　vegetable oil

1. Combine flour, baking powder, salt and pepper in medium bowl; add eggs, milk and oil. Beat with fork or small whisk until well mixed.

Makes 4 servings

India Fried Chicken

1 teaspoon (5 mL) salt
1 teaspoon (5 mL) dried
　chives
1 teaspoon (5 mL) dried
　coriander leaves
½ teaspoon (2 mL) ground
　cardamom
½ teaspoon (2 mL) paprika
¼ teaspoon (1 mL) crushed
　red pepper
⅛ teaspoon (0.5 mL) garlic
　powder
⅛ teaspoon (0.5 mL) ground
　nutmeg
⅛ teaspoon (0.5 mL) ground
　cumin
1 broiling/frying chicken
　(about 3 pounds or
　1350 g), cut into serving
　pieces, deboned and
　skinned
1 egg
¼ cup (60 mL) milk
½ cup (125 mL) all-purpose
　flour
½ cup (125 mL) fine dry
　bread crumbs
　Vegetable oil

This boneless skillet-fried chicken is seasoned with an interesting but not over-powering blend of spices. It's delicious served with steamed rice.

1. Blend salt, chives, coriander, cardamom, paprika, red pepper, garlic powder, nutmeg and cumin in small bowl.

2. Pierce chicken in several places with fork. Rub chicken with salt mixture; place on plate or in shallow pan. Cover and refrigerate 10 minutes.

3. Beat egg and milk in shallow pan. Dip chicken in flour, then dip in egg mixture. Roll chicken in bread crumbs, pressing to coat all sides evenly. Place chicken on wire rack and let dry 15 minutes.

4. Pour enough oil into large skillet to reach a level ¼-inch (0.5 cm) deep. Heat over medium-high heat until hot enough to sizzle a drop of water.

5. Cook chicken in the oil until golden, about 15 minutes. Reduce heat to low; cover and cook until chicken is tender, 30 to 40 minutes longer. Turn pieces once or twice during cooking. Uncover during last 10 minutes of cooking. Serve hot.

Roasts and Stuffings

This chapter features recipes for
traditional roasted chickens and stuffings, plus some
that may not be traditional but are truly exquisite.
They include Cordon Bleu en Cachette, Roast Chicken with
Apple Pâté, and Poulet Balle Francais.

Roast Chicken Paprikash

Makes 4 servings

1   **roasting chicken (4 to 5 pounds or 1800 to 2250 g)**
2   **tablespoons (30 mL) sour cream**
4   **teaspoons (20 mL) paprika**
1   **teaspoon (5 mL) salt**
1   **carrot, cut into 2-inch (5 cm) pieces**
1   **small onion, cut into quarters**
1   **stalk celery, cut into 2-inch (5 cm) pieces**
3   **tablespoons (45 mL) water**
   Chicken broth or water
1   **teaspoon (5 mL) cornstarch**
½   **cup (125 mL) sour cream**
   Hot buttered noodles or rice

Paprika, a favorite Hungarian seasoning, lends its sweet, sharp flavor to this roasted chicken. A luscious sour cream gravy made from the pan drippings is a pleasant complement to the chicken.

1. Heat oven to 375°F (190°C).

2. Rub outside of chicken and inside body cavity with the 2 tablespoons (30 mL) sour cream, 3 teaspoons (15 mL) of the paprika and the salt. Place carrot, onion and celery inside body cavity; tie legs together.

3. Place chicken, breast-side up, on rack in shallow roasting pan. Add 3 tablespoons (45 mL) water to pan. Roast until chicken is tender and drumstick meat feels soft when pressed with fingers, 2 to 2½ hours. Baste chicken with pan juices 3 times during roasting.

4. Remove chicken from pan and keep warm while preparing gravy.

5. Strain pan drippings; skim off fat. Add enough broth to pan drippings to measure ½ cup (125 mL).

6. Mix cornstarch, remaining 1 teaspoon (5 mL) paprika and 2 tablespoons (30 mL) of the broth mixture in small saucepan; blend in remaining broth. Cook mixture over medium heat, stirring constantly, until mixture boils. Cook, stirring constantly, until mixture is thick, about 1 minute.

7. Gradually stir 2 tablespoons (30 mL) of the hot mixture into the ½ cup (125 mL) sour cream; slowly stir sour cream into hot mixture. Remove from heat.

8. Place chicken on serving platter; remove string from legs. Serve chicken hot with noodles and gravy.

Sunday Roast Chicken

Makes 8 to 10 servings

Cranberry Stuffing (see
Index for page number)
2 roasting chickens (4 to 5
pounds or 1800 to 2250 g
each)
1 tablespoon (15 mL) salt
¼ teaspoon (1 mL) pepper
½ cup (125 mL) water
8 tablespoons (125 mL)
butter or margarine,
melted
Orange Sauce (recipe
follows)
Orange slices, if desired
Watercress or parsley, if
desired

This is a traditional family favorite. The plump, succulent chickens are filled with tangy cranberry stuffing and served with an orange sauce. The recipe yields two chickens, so there's plenty to go around.

1. Prepare Cranberry Stuffing.

2. Heat oven to 375°F (190°C).

3. Rub outsides of chickens with salt and pepper. For each chicken, pack wishbone cavity loosely with about ½ cup (125 mL) of the prepared stuffing. Close and fasten neck skin to back of chicken with metal skewer. Fold wings across back so tips touch. Pack body cavity of each chicken loosely with half of the remaining stuffing; close cavity with metal skewers. Tie legs of each chicken together.

4. Place chickens, breast-side up, on rack in shallow roasting pan; add water to pan. Brush each chicken with about 2 tablespoons (30 mL) of the butter.

5. Roast until chickens are tender and drumsticks feel soft when pressed with fingers, 2 to 2½ hours. Baste chickens with remaining butter and pan drippings 3 times during roasting.

6. While chickens are roasting, prepare Orange Sauce.

7. Place chickens on serving platter; remove skewers and strings. Garnish with orange slices and watercress. Carve chickens at table and serve with stuffing. Pass Orange Sauce.

Orange Sauce

Makes about 2½ cups (625 mL)

Rind of 1 orange, cut into
1x⅛-inch (2.5x0.5 cm)
strips
1 cup (250 mL) water
2 cups (500 mL) orange juice
⅔ cup (160 mL) light corn
syrup
2 tablespoons (30 mL)
cornstarch
1 stick cinnamon (about
2 inches or 5 cm long)
¼ teaspoon (1 mL) ground
cloves
2 tablespoons (30 mL) Grand
Marnier, if desired

1. Place orange strips and water into 2-quart (2 L) saucepan. Heat over high heat until water boils; boil 1 minute. Drain, reserving rind.

2. Combine orange juice, corn syrup, cornstarch, orange rind, cinnamon and cloves in the saucepan. Cook over medium heat, stirring constantly, until sauce boils. Stir in Grand Marnier. Cook and stir about 2 minutes longer. Keep warm until ready to serve.

ROASTS AND STUFFINGS

Cordon Bleu en Cachette

Makes 4 servings

Crusty Bread Dough
(recipe follows)
2 large whole chicken breasts, deboned and skinned
½ teaspoon (2 mL) salt
⅛ teaspoon (0.5 mL) dried dill weed
⅛ teaspoon (0.5 mL) celery salt
⅛ teaspoon (0.5 mL) pepper
3 slices Swiss Cheese (each 4x7 inches or 10x18 cm)
3 slices boiled ham (each 4x7 inches or 10x18 cm)
2 tablespoons (30 mL) butter or margarine
1 teaspoon (5 mL) butter or margarine, melted
2 teaspoons (10 mL) minced fresh parsley
1 egg white, slightly beaten
Madeira Sauce (see Index for page number)

This elegant dish is an outstanding choice for entertaining. It consists of a tender roll of chicken, ham and cheese encased in a crusty loaf of bread! The bread comes in handy for soaking up every last drop of the sauce.

1. Prepare Crusty Bread Dough as directed through second rising.

2. Meanwhile, flatten chicken by pounding between 2 pieces of wax paper until ⅛ inch (0.5 cm) thick. Remove paper. Sprinkle chicken with salt, dill, celery salt and pepper. Place chicken pieces lengthwise along side of each other, overlapping them slightly.

3. Arrange cheese slices lengthwise over chicken. Place ham over cheese slices; roll up jelly-roll fashion. Tie with string in 3 or 4 places to secure.

4. Melt the 2 tablespoons (30 mL) butter in large skillet over medium heat. Cook chicken roll in the butter on all sides until golden, about 2 minutes on each side.

5. Punch down Crusty Bread Dough. Roll out dough into a 10x12-inch (25x30 cm) rectangle. Brush dough with 1 teaspoon (5 mL) melted butter. Sprinkle dough with parsley. Remove strings from chicken roll. Place roll lengthwise down center of dough. Fold dough over chicken and pinch seam to seal well. Fold dough over ends of chicken. Pinch seam to seal.

6. Place dough, seam-side down, on greased cookie sheet. Cover loosely with plastic wrap. Let stand in warm place (85°F or 30°C) until doubled, about 45 minutes.

7. Heat oven to 375°F (190°C). Brush dough with egg white. Bake 15 minutes. Reduce temperature to 350°F (180°C). Bake until bread is golden, 20 to 25 minutes longer.

8. Prepare Madeira Sauce while bread is baking.

9. To serve, remove bread from chicken. Tear bread into serving pieces; cut chicken into serving portions. Pour a third of the Madeira Sauce over the chicken. Serve hot with remaining sauce and the bread.

Crusty Bread Dough

2 to 2¼ cups (500 to 560 mL) all-purpose flour
1 package (¼ ounce or 7 g) active dry yeast
⅔ cup (160 mL) water
1 tablespoon (15 mL) butter or margarine
1 teaspoon (5 mL) sugar
1 teaspoon (5 mL) salt
1 egg yolk

1. Stir ½ cup (125 mL) of the flour and the yeast in medium bowl.

2. Combine water, butter, sugar and salt in 1-quart (1 L) saucepan. Cook over low heat only until warm (120° to 130°F or 49° to 54°C).

3. Add water mixture and egg yolk to flour-yeast mixture. Beat until smooth, about 2 minutes on medium speed of electric mixer or 300 strokes by hand. Add ½ cup (125 mL) of the flour. Beat 1 minute on medium speed or 150 strokes by hand.

4. Cover bowl loosely with plastic wrap and let stand in warm place (85°F or 30°C) until light and bubbly, about 45 minutes. *continued*

Crusty Bread Dough (continued)

5. Stir down batter. Gradually stir in enough remaining flour to make a moderately stiff dough.

6. Turn dough onto lightly floured surface. Knead until smooth and satiny and small bubbles form under the surface, 10 to 15 minutes.

7. Shape dough into ball and place in lightly greased bowl, turning to grease all sides. Cover loosely with plastic wrap and let stand in warm place until doubled, about 1 hour. Shape and bake as directed for Cordon Bleu en Cachette.

Makes 4 servings

Burgundy Rock Cornish Hens

4   **frozen Rock Cornish hens, thawed (1 to 1½ pounds or 450 to 675 g each) Cold water**
1   **teaspoon (5 mL) salt**
⅛   **teaspoon (0.5 mL) pepper**
8   **tablespoons (125 mL) butter or margarine, melted**
¼   **cup (60 mL) water**
2   **tablespoons (30 mL) toasted slivered almonds Burgundy Fruit Sauce (recipe follows)**

Served with Burgundy Fruit Sauce, these handsome little hens are nice for a special family dinner or a gathering of guests. Wild rice, crisp leafy green salads and buttery croissants would be perfect choices to serve with the hens.

1. Heat oven to 425°F (220°C).

2. Remove giblets from inside of each hen; discard giblets or reserve for another use. Rinse hens with cold water and drain on paper toweling. Fold wings across the back so tips touch; tie legs together. Rub each hen with salt and pepper; brush outside of each hen with 1 tablespoon (15 mL) of the butter.

3. Place hens, breast-side up, in shallow roasting pan; add ¼ cup (60 mL) water to pan. Bake until hens are tender, about 1 hour. Baste hens with remaining 4 tablespoons (60 mL) butter every 15 minutes during roasting.

4. Prepare Burgundy Fruit Sauce.

5. Place hens on serving plates; remove strings from legs. Pour sauce over hens; sprinkle with almonds. Serve hot.

Makes about 2 cups (500 mL)

Burgundy Fruit Sauce

1   **can (17 ounces or 480 g) fruit cocktail Water**
2   **tablespoons (30 mL) cornstarch**
2   **tablespoons (30 mL) sugar**
2   **tablespoons (30 mL) butter or margarine**
1   **cup (250 mL) burgundy wine**

1. Drain fruit, reserving fruit and juice. Add enough water to juice to measure 1 cup (250 mL).

2. Mix cornstarch and sugar in 1-quart (1 L) saucepan; blend in reserved juice and water mixture. Cook over medium heat, stirring constantly, until mixture boils. Add butter and wine. Boil and stir 1 to 2 minutes.

3. Stir fruit into thickened sauce. Cook and stir until fruit is hot, about 2 minutes longer.

ROASTS AND STUFFINGS

Makes 4 servings

Broiled Rock Cornish Hens

Barbecue Sauce, if desired
(see Index for page
number)
Spiced Fruit, if desired (see
Index for page number)
4   frozen Rock Cornish hens,
thawed (1 to 1½ pounds
or 450 to 675 g each)
1   teaspoon (5 mL) salt
Pinch pepper
½   cup (125 mL) butter or
margarine, melted

Quick to cook indoors or outdoors, these Cornish hens can be brushed with barbecue sauce and garnished with spiced fruit for a fun and easy meal.

1. Prepare Barbecue Sauce.

2. Prepare Spiced Fruit.

3. Remove giblets from inside of each hen; discard giblets or reserve for another use. Cut each bird into halves lengthwise along backbone and down center of breast; remove and discard backbones. Rinse hens with water; drain on paper toweling. Fasten wings to body with skewers.

4. Sprinkle hens with salt and pepper; place, skin-side down, on broiler pan. Brush with butter.

5. Broil about 5 inches (13 cm) from heat until hens are golden, about 15 minutes. Turn hens over; brush with butter. Broil until hens are golden, about 15 minutes longer. (If using Barbecue Sauce, brush hens with sauce during last 7 minutes of broiling.) Serve hens hot, garnished with Spiced Fruit.

To Cook on Outdoor Grill
Place hen halves, skin-side up, on greased charcoal grill over hot coals. Broil about 6 inches (15 cm) from heat, basting frequently with butter; turn hens over every 5 to 8 minutes. Cook until hens are tender and golden on both sides, 25 to 30 minutes. (If using Barbecue Sauce, brush hens with sauce during last 5 minutes of grilling.)

Makes 4 servings

Roast Chicken with Apple Pâté

⅓   cup (80 mL) golden raisins
⅓   cup (80 mL) dry sherry
⅓   cup (80 mL) blanched
whole almonds
2   cups (500 mL) chopped,
peeled apple (about
2 medium apples)
¾   cup (180 mL) fine dry
bread crumbs
2   tablespoons (30 mL) butter
or margarine
2   teaspoons (10 mL) grated
Parmesan cheese
1   roasting chicken (4 to
5 pounds or 1800 to
2250 g) *continued*

A pâté of ground almonds, apples, and raisins makes a delectable stuffing that is tucked under the skin of the chicken before roasting.

1. Place raisins in small bowl; pour sherry over raisins. Let stand about 15 minutes.

2. Place almonds in food processor container and chop finely or place in food grinder and grind.

3. Add apple, bread crumbs, the 2 tablespoons (30 mL) butter, the cheese and the raisin-sherry mixture to almonds. Process or grind until mixture is thoroughly blended and resembles a pâté in texture. Reserve.

4. Heat oven to 350°F (180°C).

5. Sprinkle chicken with ½ teaspoon (2 mL) of the salt and ⅛ teaspoon (0.5 mL) of the pepper. Rub body cavity with remaining ½ teaspoon (2 mL) salt and ⅛ teaspoon (0.5 mL) pepper.

Roast Chicken with Apple Pâté *(continued)*

1   **teaspoon (5 mL) salt**
¼   **teaspoon (1 mL) white pepper**
1   **tablespoon (15 mL) butter or margarine, melted**
⅓   **cup (80 mL) water**

6. Place chicken breast-side up on work surface. Carefully loosen skin from one side of breast toward the wing, then loosen skin around leg. Repeat to loosen skin on other side of chicken. Do not tear skin.

7. Gently push about ⅓ cup (80 mL) of the stuffing under the skin of 1 leg with fingers of one hand; mold the outside of the skin with the other hand. Repeat procedure with other leg.

8. Gently push about ⅔ cup (160 mL) of the remaining stuffing under skin of breast on each side; mold the outside of the skin.

9. Tuck neck skin under chicken; fold wings across back so tips touch. Fasten skin across body cavity with skewers. Tie drumsticks together.

10. Place chicken, breast-side up, on rack in shallow roasting pan. Brush skin with melted butter; pour the water into pan. Cover chicken with aluminum foil.

11. Roast chicken 1 hour. Remove foil; roast until chicken is tender and drumstick meat feels soft when pressed with fingers, 1 to 1½ hours longer. Baste chicken with pan juices 3 times during roasting.

12. Place chicken on platter; remove string and skewers. Serve hot.

Makes 4 to 6 servings

Poulet with Forty Cloves of Garlic

1   **roasting chicken (4 to 5 pounds or 1800 to 2250 g)**
1   **teaspoon (5 mL) salt**
½   **teaspoon (2 mL) pepper**
¼   **teaspoon (1 mL) dried thyme leaves**
⅛   **teaspoon (0.5 mL) dried rosemary leaves**
1   **stalk celery (including leaves), cut into 4 pieces**
1   **carrot, cut lengthwise into 4 pieces**
3   **thin slices lemon**
1   **fresh parsley sprig**
40 **cloves garlic, whole, unpeeled (about 1½ bulbs)**
2   **tablespoons (30 mL) olive or vegetable oil**
     Sliced French bread, if desired

Surprisingly enough, the lavish amount of garlic used in this recipe actually adds an enticing sweet flavor to roasted chicken. In France, where this dish originated, the soft cooked garlic cloves are spread over warm crusty bread and eaten with the succulent chicken.

1. Soak top and bottom of 3¼-quart (3.25 L) clay cooker in cool tap water 15 minutes.

2. Rub outside of chicken with salt and pepper; rub inside body cavity with thyme and rosemary.

3. Place 2 pieces celery, 2 pieces carrot, 1 slice lemon and the parsley inside body cavity. Tie legs together.

4. Arrange remaining 2 pieces celery, 2 pieces carrot and 2 slices lemon over bottom of clay cooker. Place chicken over vegetables and lemon in cooker.

5. Sprinkle garlic around chicken; drizzle oil over chicken.

6. Cover cooker and place in cold oven; set oven at 425°F (220°C). Bake until chicken is golden and tender, about 1¼ hours.

7. Place chicken on serving platter; arrange garlic cloves around chicken. Serve hot with French bread.

ROASTS AND STUFFINGS

Makes 4 servings

Poulet Balle Francais

Basic Bread Stuffing (see Index for page number)
1   broiling/frying chicken (about 3½ pounds or 1600 g)
1   teaspoon (5 mL) salt
¼   teaspoon (1 mL) pepper
2   tablespoons (30 mL) butter or margarine, at room temperature
¼   cup (60 mL) chablis wine
2   cups (500 mL) Bordelaise Sauce (see Index for page number)
    Kumquats, if desired
    Fresh parsley, if desired

This is a marvelous dish for entertaining! It is a boneless chicken stuffed with a bread dressing, basted with butter and chablis during roasting and served with a sensational Bordelaise Sauce.

1. Prepare Basic Bread Stuffing.

2. Debone chicken, deboning legs and removing wings (see Preparation Techniques).

3. Heat oven to 375°F (190°C).

4. Place deboned chicken skin-side down on work surface; sprinkle with salt and pepper. Place stuffing into center of chicken. Bring the 2 sides of chicken together over stuffing; press legs flat against sides. Fasten skin with metal skewers or wooden picks. Bring neck and tail ends together and fasten skin with skewers.

5. Turn chicken over and gently shape into ball; place in greased 9-inch (23 cm) square baking pan. Cut a piece of aluminum foil long enough to wrap completely around base of chicken. Fold foil into 1-inch (2.5 cm) wide strip; place foil in ring around base of chicken. Tuck foil ends under chicken. Rub chicken with 1 tablespoon (15 mL) of the butter. Pour chablis over chicken.

6. Roast until chicken is tender, about 1½ hours. Baste chicken with remaining 1 tablespoon (15 mL) butter and the pan juices 4 times during roasting.

7. While chicken is roasting, prepare Bordelaise Sauce.

8. Place chicken on serving platter; remove aluminum foil and skewers. Cut chicken into 1-inch (2.5 cm) thick slices. Garnish with kumquats and parsley. Serve hot with Bordelaise Sauce.

Makes 4 to 6 servings

Stuffed Boneless Bird

Crabmeat Stuffing or Basic Bread Stuffing (see Index for page numbers)
1   broiling/frying chicken (about 3 pounds or 1350 g) or roasting chicken (about 4 to 5 pounds or 1800 to 2250 g)
½   teaspoon (2 mL) salt
⅛   teaspoon (0.5 mL) pepper
    continued

One of the most impressive poultry dishes you can choose, this deboned chicken is stuffed with a delicate crabmeat dressing before roasting.

1. Prepare Crabmeat Stuffing or Basic Bread Stuffing.

2. Debone chicken leaving wings and drumsticks intact (see Preparation Techniques).

3. Heat oven to 375°F (190°C).

4. Place chicken, skin-side down, on work surface; sprinkle with salt and pepper. Place Crabmeat Stuffing lengthwise down center of chicken.

5. Bring 2 sides of chicken together; fasten skin together by inserting an

Stuffed Boneless Bird *(continued)*

2	tablespoons (30 mL) butter or margarine, at room temperature
¼	cup (60 mL) dry red wine

8-inch (20 cm) metal skewer lengthwise in a lacing fashion through the skin. Fasten skin at neck end using small metal skewer; fasten skin at tail end with skewer.

6. Turn chicken over; reshape to resemble a chicken. Tie legs together.

7. Place chicken in shallow roasting pan. Rub chicken with 1 tablespoon (15 mL) of the butter; pour wine into roasting pan. Roast until chicken is golden, about 1½ hours. Baste chicken with remaining 1 tablespoon (15 mL) butter and the pan juices 4 times during roasting.

8. Place chicken on serving platter; remove wings, skewers and string from legs. Cut chicken crosswise into slices about 1 inch (2.5 cm) thick. Serve hot.

Chicken in Solitaire

Makes 4 to 6 servings

1½	teaspoons (7 mL) salt
¼	teaspoon (1 mL) pepper
⅛	teaspoon (0.5 mL) paprika
1	broiling/frying chicken (about 3 pounds or 1350 g)
2	pieces (2 inches or 5 cm long each) celery
1	can (8 ounces or 225 g) tomatoes
2	tablespoons (30 mL) Madeira wine
¼	teaspoon (1 mL) ground cinnamon
½	orange, cut into quarters
1	clove garlic, cut into halves
1	cup (250 mL) all-purpose flour
7	tablespoons (105 mL) water
2	teaspoons (10 mL) cornstarch
½	teaspoon (2 mL) sugar
6	pitted ripe olives, sliced Hot cooked rice

This piquant chicken bakes in a covered casserole dish that is sealed with pastry to lock in the savory flavors.

1. Mix salt, pepper and paprika in small bowl; rub chicken with salt mixture. Place celery in cavity of chicken; tie legs together. Place chicken in 3-quart (3 L) baking dish with cover.

2. Mix tomatoes, Madeira and cinnamon in small bowl; pour around chicken. Place 2 orange quarters and ½ clove garlic on each side of chicken. Cover baking dish.

3. Combine flour and 6 tablespoons (90 mL) of the water in small bowl. Spread strip of flour mixture around baking dish and its cover, sealing the two together.

4. Place dish in cold oven; set oven at 425°F (220°C). Bake 1 hour and 20 minutes. Remove dish from oven; let stand 5 minutes.

5. Crack off dough carefully, using wooden mallet or wooden spoon; discard dough.

6. Remove chicken from dish and place on serving platter; remove string from legs and celery from inside cavity. Reserve chicken.

7. Strain tomato mixture from baking dish into 1-quart (1 L) saucepan.

8. Blend cornstarch, sugar and remaining 1 tablespoon (15 mL) water in small bowl. Blend ¼ cup (60 mL) of the tomato mixture into cornstarch mixture; stir cornstarch mixture into remaining tomato mixture. Add olives to tomato mixture. Cook over medium heat until mixture boils, 1 to 2 minutes. Boil 1 minute longer; remove from heat.

9. Serve chicken hot with gravy and rice.

ROASTS AND STUFFINGS

Makes 4 servings

Chicken Stuffed with Rice

Rice Stuffing (see Index for page number)
1 teaspoon (5 mL) salt
¼ teaspoon (1 mL) celery salt
¼ teaspoon (1 mL) pepper
¼ teaspoon (1 mL) ground sage
1 roasting chicken (4 to 5 pounds or 1800 to 2250 g)
4 tablespoons (60 mL) butter or margarine, melted
½ cup (125 mL) water
8 ounces (225 g) mushroom caps
1 small lemon, cut into 8 wedges, if desired

Tender roast chicken becomes extraordinary when it is filled with a special raisin-rice stuffing. A border of buttered mushrooms and lemon wedges makes a pretty garnish for this succulent entrée.

1. Prepare Rice Stuffing.

2. Heat oven to 375°F (190°C).

3. Mix salt, celery salt, pepper and sage in small bowl; rub chicken with mixture.

4. Pack wishbone cavity of chicken loosely with about ½ cup (125 mL) of the Rice Stuffing; close and fasten neck skin to back of chicken using metal skewer. Fold wings across back so tips touch. Pack body cavity loosely with remaining stuffing. Tie legs together.

5. Place chicken, breast-side up, on rack in shallow roasting pan. Brush 2 tablespoons (30 mL) of the butter over chicken. Pour water into pan. Roast until chicken is tender and drumstick meat feels soft when pressed with fingers, 2 to 2½ hours. Baste chicken with pan drippings 3 times during roasting. Place chicken on serving platter; remove string from legs.

6. Melt remaining 2 tablespoons (30 mL) butter in skillet; add mushrooms. Cook over medium heat, stirring frequently, until mushrooms are light brown, about 5 minutes. Spoon mushrooms around chicken. Garnish with lemon. Serve hot.

Makes 6 to 10 servings

Roast Capon

1 capon (5 to 7 pounds or 2250 to 3150 g)
1½ tablespoons (22 mL) lemon juice
½ teaspoon (2 mL) salt
⅛ teaspoon (0.5 mL) pepper
3 pieces (2 inches or 5 cm long each) celery
4 tablespoons (60 mL) butter or margarine, at room temperature
Pan Gravy (recipe follows)

This bird is prepared in the same manner as chicken and served with its own delicious pan gravy.

1. Heat oven to 450°F (230°C).

2. Rub outside of capon and inside body cavity with lemon juice, salt and pepper. Place celery inside body cavity; tie legs together. Rub outside of chicken with 1 tablespoon (15 mL) of the butter.

3. Place capon, breast-side up, on rack in shallow roasting pan. Roast 30 minutes. Reduce oven temperature to 375°F (190°C). Roast until capon is tender and drumstick meat feels soft when pressed with fingers, 1½ to 2 hours longer. Baste with remaining 3 tablespoons (45 mL) butter and pan drippings 3 or 4 times during roasting.

4. Place capon on large serving platter. Remove string from legs and celery from inside cavity. Keep capon warm.

5. Prepare Pan Gravy. Serve capon with gravy.

Pan Gravy

Makes 2 cups (500 mL)

¼ cup (60 mL) pan drippings
    Butter or margarine, melted
¼ cup (60 mL) all-purpose
    flour
½ teaspoon (2 mL) celery salt
    Pepper, if desired
2 cups (500 mL) chicken
    juices, broth and/or
    water

1. Pour pan drippings into measuring cup, leaving crusty brown particles in roasting pan. Add butter, if necessary, to measure ¼ cup (60 mL); return drippings to pan.

2. Stir flour, celery salt and pepper into pan drippings. Cook over low heat, stirring constantly, until bubbly; remove from heat.

3. Pour flour mixture into 2-quart (2 L) saucepan; blend in liquid. Cook over medium heat, stirring constantly, until mixture boils; boil, stirring occasionally, 3 to 5 minutes. Serve hot.

Chicken Legs Florentine

Makes 4 servings

1 package (10 ounces or
    285 g) frozen chopped
    spinach
4 tablespoons (60 mL) butter
    or margarine
¼ cup (60 mL) chopped
    onion
⅓ cup (80 mL) shredded
    Swiss or Mozzarella
    cheese
3 tablespoons (45 mL) grated
    Parmesan or Romano
    cheese
1 egg, slightly beaten
¼ teaspoon (1 mL) salt
⅛ teaspoon (0.5 mL) ground
    nutmeg
⅛ teaspoon (0.5 mL) pepper
4 whole chicken legs,
    deboned
⅓ cup (80 mL) dry red wine

An inexpensive yet elegant way to serve chicken, whole legs are deboned and filled with a savory spinach and cheese stuffing. If desired, other stuffings could be used.

1. Heat oven to 400°F (200°C).

2. Cook spinach according to package directions; drain. Cool slightly; squeeze out excess liquid. Reserve.

3. Melt 2 tablespoons (30 mL) of the butter in small skillet; add onion. Cook until onion is soft, about 3 minutes.

4. Combine onion, spinach, cheeses, egg, salt, nutmeg and pepper in medium bowl; mix well.

5. Place deboned legs, skin-side down, on work surface. Place small piece of waxed paper over each leg; flatten each leg slightly by pounding. Place about ¼ cup (60 mL) of the spinach mixture onto center of each leg. Fold edges of chicken over spinach mixture; press chicken into ball. Fasten skin together with small metal skewers or wooden picks.

6. Place chicken, skin-side up, in greased 9-inch (23 cm) square baking dish.

7. Brush remaining 2 tablespoons (30 mL) butter over chicken. Pour wine over chicken. Bake until chicken is tender, 45 to 55 minutes. Baste chicken with pan juices 2 or 3 times during cooking.

8. Remove skewers from chicken; place chicken on serving plate. Spoon pan juices over chicken. Serve hot.

ROASTS AND STUFFINGS

Sangria Chicken

1	roasting chicken (4 to 5 pounds or 1800 to 2250 g)
6	orange slices (each about ⅛ inch or 0.5 cm thick)
3	lemon slices (each about ⅛ inch or 0.5 cm thick)
3	tablespoons (45 mL) chablis wine
1	teaspoon (5 mL) salt
⅛	teaspoon (0.5 mL) pepper
2	pieces celery (each 2 inches or 5 cm long)
2	tablespoons (30 mL) butter or margarine, at room temperature
½	cup (125 mL) water
	Chicken broth
2	tablespoons (30 mL) all-purpose flour
¼	teaspoon (1 mL) sugar

Mixing wine with fruit in the Spanish beverage Sangria provided the inspiration for this continental recipe. Thin lemon and orange slices are carefully tucked under the skin of the chicken before roasting.

1. Heat oven to 375°F (190°C).

2. Place chicken, breast-side up, on work surface. Carefully loosen skin from flesh with fingers, starting above the body cavity near breast bone. Work from one side of breast toward wing, then loosen skin around leg. Repeat to loosen skin on other side of chicken. Do not tear skin.

3. Carefully slide 2 of the orange slices and 1 of the lemon slices under skin on each side of breast and leg.

4. Rub body cavity of chicken with 1 tablespoon (15 mL) of the chablis, the salt and pepper. Place celery, remaining 2 orange slices and the remaining lemon slice inside cavity.

5. Brush outside of chicken evenly with butter. Fold wings across back so tips touch; tie legs together.

6. Place chicken, breast-side up, on rack in shallow roasting pan. Pour water and remaining 2 tablespoons (30 mL) chablis into pan.

7. Roast until chicken is tender and drumstick meat feels soft when pressed with fingers, 2 to 2½ hours. Baste chicken with pan juices 3 times during roasting.

8. Remove chicken from roasting pan and keep warm while preparing gravy. Place chicken on serving platter; remove string.

9. Pour pan drippings into measuring cup. Skim off fat; return 2 tablespoons (30 mL) of the fat to the roasting pan. Discard remaining fat. Add enough broth to pan drippings to measure 1 cup (250 mL); reserve.

10. Stir flour into fat in roasting pan. Cook over low heat, stirring constantly, until mixture bubbles, 1 to 2 minutes. Slowly stir broth mixture into flour mixture; add sugar. Cook over medium heat, stirring constantly, until mixture boils, about 5 minutes. Boil 1 minute longer. Serve chicken hot with gravy.

Glazed Cornish Hens

Makes 4 servings

Festive and attractive for entertaining, these little hens are stuffed with wild rice and mushrooms and served with a spicy currant jelly glaze.

Wild Rice Stuffing (see Index for page number)
4   frozen Rock Cornish hens, thawed (1 to 1½ pounds or 450 to 675 g each)
Cold water
¼   cup (60 mL) chicken broth
½   teaspoon (2 mL) salt
⅛   teaspoon (0.5 mL) pepper
8   tablespoons (120 mL) butter or margarine
¼   cup (60 mL) water
Spicy Jelly Glaze (recipe follows)
Fresh parsley, if desired
Crab apples, if desired

1. Prepare Wild Rice Stuffing.

2. Heat oven to 425°F (220°C).

3. Remove giblets from inside of each hen; discard giblets or reserve for another use. Rinse hens with cold water; drain on paper toweling.

4. Stuff body cavity of each hen with ½ cup (125 mL) of the Wild Rice Stuffing; place remaining stuffing in greased 1-quart (1 L) baking dish. Pour broth over stuffing in dish; cover and reserve.

5. Close body of each hen with metal skewers. Tie legs of each hen together.

6. Rub hens with salt and pepper; brush outside of each hen with 1 tablespoon (15 mL) of the melted butter.

7. Place hens, breast-side up, in shallow roasting pan. Add ¼ cup (60 mL) water to pan.

8. Roast until hens are tender, about 1 hour. Baste hens with remaining butter every 15 minutes during roasting.

9. While hens are roasting, prepare Spiced Jelly Glaze.

10. About 25 minutes before hens are done, place reserved stuffing in oven; bake, covered, until done, 20 to 25 minutes.

11. Place hens on serving plates; brush with glaze. Garnish hens with parsley and crab apples. Pass remaining glaze.

Spicy Jelly Glaze

Makes about ⅔ cup (160 mL)

1   tablespoon (15 mL) butter or margarine
⅔   cup (160 mL) currant jelly
¼   cup (60 mL) grenadine syrup
2   tablespoons (30 mL) lemon juice
2   teaspoons (10 mL) vinegar
1   tablespoon (15 mL) cornstarch
½   teaspoon (2 mL) salt
4   whole cloves

1. Melt butter in 1-quart (1 L) saucepan over medium heat; add jelly, grenadine and 1 tablespoon (15 mL) of the lemon juice. Cook over low heat, stirring constantly, until jelly melts. Remove from heat and reserve.

2. Blend remaining 1 tablespoon (15 mL) lemon juice, the vinegar and cornstarch in small bowl; stir into jelly mixture. Add salt and cloves to jelly mixture. Cook, stirring constantly, until mixture boils and thickens. Boil 1 minute. Remove cloves before serving.

ROASTS AND STUFFINGS

Makes 4 to 6 servings

Spit-Roasted Chicken

Pacific Barbecue Sauce (see Index for page number)
1 roasting chicken (4 to 5 pounds or 1800 to 2250 g) or 2 broiling/frying chickens (about 2 pounds or 900 g each)
2 tablespoons (30 mL) dry white wine
1 teaspoon (5 mL) salt
½ teaspoon (2 mL) pepper
Vegetable oil or butter or margarine, melted

Basted with a zesty barbecue sauce, this tasty chicken is roasted outdoors on an electric rotisserie.

1. Prepare Pacific Barbecue Sauce.

2. Rub inside body cavity of chicken with wine; rub inside body cavity and outside of chicken with salt and pepper.

3. Fasten neck skin to back of bird with metal skewer. Fold wings across back so tips touch; tie close to body with string. Fasten skin across body cavity with metal skewers. Tie string firmly onto tail; tie legs securely.

4. Fasten chicken onto spit of rotisserie according to manufacturer's directions. Check to be certain poultry is well-balanced on spit.

5. Brush chicken with oil. Insert tip of thermometer into meaty part of thigh or into center of stuffing if bird is stuffed.

6. Attach spit to rotisserie according to manufacturer's directions. Cook over medium heat until internal temperature of chicken registers 180°F (85°C) on the thermometer, 1¼ to 1¾ hours if unstuffed. If chicken is stuffed, cook about 20 minutes longer. Brush chicken with oil several times during cooking. Baste with Pacific Barbecue Sauce several times during last 20 minutes of cooking. Remove chicken from spit; serve hot with remaining sauce.

Makes about 3 cups (750 mL)

Rice Stuffing

1½ cups (375 mL) water
¾ cup (180 mL) uncooked rice
½ teaspoon (2 mL) salt
2 tablespoons (30 mL) butter or margarine
½ pound (225 g) lean ground beef
⅓ cup (80 mL) chopped celery
¼ cup (60 mL) chopped onion
⅓ cup (80 mL) dark raisins
2 teaspoons (10 mL) instant chicken bouillon granules
2 teaspoons (10 mL) minced fresh parsley
½ teaspoon (2 mL) ground sage
½ teaspoon (2 mL) celery salt
¼ teaspoon (1 mL) pepper

Combining rice with seasoned ground beef and raisins creates a robust stuffing for a roasting chicken.

1. Heat water in 2-quart (2 L) saucepan over high heat until boiling; stir in rice and ¼ teaspoon (1 mL) of the salt. Reduce heat; cover and cook until rice is done, about 15 minutes. Remove from heat; reserve.

2. Melt butter in large skillet over medium heat; add beef, celery and onion. Cook, stirring occasionally, until meat browns, 5 to 7 minutes.

3. Add rice, raisins, bouillon, parsley, sage, celery salt, pepper and remaining ¼ teaspoon (1 mL) salt to meat mixture; mix well.

4. Stuff in poultry, as desired, or bake separately (see Chicken Preparation Tips).

Dilly Rice Stuffing
Prepare as directed for Rice Stuffing, omitting raisins, sage and celery salt and adding 1 teaspoon (5 mL) dried dill weed.

Curried Rice Stuffing
Prepare as directed for Rice Stuffing, omitting sage and celery salt and adding 1 teaspoon (5 mL) curry powder.

Glazed Cornish Hens

Ratatouille Stir-Fry

Batter Fried Chicken

Roast Chicken Paprikash

Chicken Marengo

Stuffed Boneless Bird

Chicken Skillet Supper

Teddi's Pan Dressing

Makes about 12 servings

3   packages (12 ounces or 340 g each) brown-and-serve rolls
    Heart, gizzard, neck and liver from 5 to 7 pound (2250 to 3150 mL) roasting chicken or capon
½   stalk celery, cut into 2-inch (5 cm) pieces
½   small onion
1   clove garlic, cut into halves
    Water
1   cup (250 mL) butter or margarine
1½ cups (750 mL) chopped onion
1½ cups (750 mL) chopped celery
2   teaspoons (10 mL) ground sage
1   teaspoon (5 mL) pepper
¼   teaspoon (1 mL) salt
3   eggs, slightly beaten
1   can (44 ounces or 1240 g) chicken broth

This marvelous dressing is baked in a pan. It's good with any roasted poultry and is especially nice to serve at big holiday dinners when there never seems to be enough stuffing to go around!

1. Bake rolls according to package directions several hours or the night before needed. Let stand uncovered at least 3 hours to dry.

2. Place heart, gizzard, neck, celery pieces, ½ onion and the garlic in 2-quart (2 L) saucepan; add enough water to cover. Cook over medium-high heat until water boils. Reduce heat to low; cover and cook until giblets are tender, 1½ to 2 hours. Add liver; cook 15 minutes longer.

3. Drain giblets and cool to lukewarm. Discard neck and cooked vegetables; chop remaining giblets.

4. Melt butter in large skillet over medium heat; add chopped onion, chopped celery and chopped giblets. Cook until onion is soft, about 3 minutes. Mix in sage, pepper and salt; remove from heat.

5. Tear rolls into small pieces and place in large bowl; add eggs, giblet mixture and broth. Toss lightly until well mixed. Place dressing in greased 13x9x2-inch (33x23x5 cm) baking pan; cover with aluminum foil. Refrigerate overnight, if desired.

6. Heat oven to 400°F (200°C). Bake dressing 1 hour. Remove aluminum foil; bake until dressing is golden, about 20 minutes longer. Serve hot.

Cranberry Stuffing

Makes about 4 cups (1 L)

1   package (8 ounces or 225 g) herb-seasoned bread stuffing
1   cup (250 mL) cranberry-orange relish
½   cup (125 mL) chopped walnuts
⅓   cup (80 mL) dark raisins
½   teaspoon (2 mL) salt
⅛   teaspoon (0.5 mL) ground cinnamon
¾   cup (180 mL) chicken broth
½   cup (125 mL) butter or margarine

This unusual cranberry stuffing is studded with crunchy walnuts and plump raisins. It's perfect with roasted poultry for the holidays.

1. Place stuffing, relish, walnuts, raisins, salt and cinnamon in large bowl; toss lightly.

2. Place broth and butter in small saucepan; cook over high heat until broth boils and butter melts.

3. Pour broth mixture over stuffing mixture; toss lightly until mixed.

4. Stuff in poultry, as desired, or bake separately (see Chicken Preparation Tips).

ROASTS AND STUFFINGS

Corn Bread Stuffing

Makes about 4 cups (1 L)

8	ounces (225 g) bulk pork sausage
¼	cup (60 mL) butter or margarine
½	cup (125 mL) chopped onion
½	cup (125 mL) chopped celery
¼	cup (60 mL) finely chopped green pepper
3	cups (750 mL) crumbled corn bread
2	cups (500 mL) dried fresh bread cubes*
⅔	cup (160 mL) chicken broth
1	egg, slightly beaten
½	teaspoon (2 mL) ground sage
½	teaspoon (2 mL) dried thyme leaves
¼	teaspoon (1 mL) salt
⅛	teaspoon (0.5 mL) ground pepper

Pork sausage contributes a rich, hearty taste to this old-fashioned Southern-style stuffing.

1. Place sausage in medium skillet; break into small pieces with fork. Cook sausage over medium heat, stirring frequently, until light brown, about 10 minutes.

2. Add butter, onion, celery and green pepper to sausage; cook until onion is soft, about 3 minutes. Remove from heat; cool slightly.

3. Place pork mixture and all remaining ingredients in large bowl; toss lightly until mixed.

4. Stuff in poultry, as desired, or bake separately (see Chicken Preparation Tips).

*Note: To prepare cubes, cut 1 or 2 day-old bread into ½-inch (1.5 cm) cubes. Let cubes stand uncovered overnight to dry.

Prune and Apple Stuffing

Makes about 4 cups (1 L)

½	cup (125 mL) pitted prunes Hot water
4	cups (1 L) soft bread cubes
1	large apple, peeled and diced
1	tablespoon (15 mL) finely chopped onion
½	teaspoon (2 mL) salt
½	teaspoon (2 mL) ground sage
⅛	teaspoon (0.5 mL) dried summer savory leaves
⅛	teaspoon (0.5 mL) dried thyme leaves
⅛	teaspoon (0.5 mL) dried marjoram leaves
2	tablespoons (30 mL) butter or margarine, melted

The distinctive flavors of prunes and apples make an enticing combination for this moist stuffing.

1. Place prunes in small bowl; add enough hot water to cover prunes. Let prunes stand 10 minutes; drain and chop coarsely.

2. Place prunes and all remaining ingredients in large bowl; toss lightly until mixed.

3. Stuff in poultry, as desired, or bake separately (see Chicken Preparation Tips).

Easy Sage Stuffing

Makes about 4 cups (1 L)

- ⅓ cup (80 mL) butter or margarine
- 1 cup (250 mL) chopped celery
- 1 cup (250 mL) sliced mushrooms
- ½ cup (125 mL) chopped onion
- ¾ cup (180 mL) plus 2 tablespoons (30 mL) water
- ½ package (14-ounce or 400 g size) dried bread stuffing cubes
- ¼ cup (60 mL) minced fresh parsley
- ½ teaspoon (2 mL) ground sage
- ½ teaspoon (2 mL) dried thyme leaves
- ¼ teaspoon (1 mL) pepper

This sage-seasoned stuffing is easy to make with convenient packaged stuffing cubes.

1. Melt butter in large skillet over medium heat; add celery, mushrooms and onion. Cook until onion is soft, about 3 minutes.

2. Pour water into skillet and heat until warm. Remove from heat.

3. Place remaining ingredients in large mixing bowl; add water mixture and toss lightly until mixed.

4. Stuff in poultry, as desired, or bake separately (see Chicken Preparation Tips).

Basic Bread Stuffing

Makes about 3 cups (750 mL)

- ¼ cup (60 mL) butter or margarine
- ⅓ cup (80 mL) chopped celery
- ¼ cup (60 mL) finely chopped onion
- 3 cups (750 mL) dried fresh bread cubes*
- ½ teaspoon (2 mL) poultry seasoning or 1¼ teaspoons (6 mL) ground sage
- ¼ teaspoon (1 mL) salt
- ¼ teaspoon (1 mL) pepper
- ¼ cup (60 mL) water or chicken broth

Good with any poultry, this traditional stuffing is easy to prepare and tastes wonderful.

1. Melt butter in small skillet over medium heat; add celery and onion. Cook until onion is soft, about 3 minutes.

2. Place celery mixture and all remaining ingredients in large bowl; toss lightly until mixed.

3. Stuff in poultry, as desired, or bake separately (see Chicken Preparation Tips).

*Note: To prepare cubes, cut 1 or 2 day-old bread into ½-inch (1.5 cm) cubes. Let cubes stand uncovered overnight to dry.

ROASTS AND STUFFINGS

Crabmeat Stuffing

Makes about 4 cups (1 L)

¼ cup (60 mL) butter or margarine
½ cup (125 mL) chopped celery
¼ cup (60 mL) thinly sliced green onions
6 cups (1.5 L) soft bread crumbs
1 package (6 ounces or 170 g) frozen crabmeat, thawed, drained and flaked
2 tablespoons (30 mL) grated carrot
¼ teaspoon (1 mL) dried marjoram leaves
¼ teaspoon (1 mL) dried dill weed
⅛ teaspoon (0.5 mL) salt
⅛ teaspoon (0.5 mL) garlic powder
⅛ teaspoon (0.5 mL) pepper

Different from most stuffings, this moist crabmeat stuffing will complement any roast poultry.

1. Melt butter in small skillet over medium heat; add celery and onion. Cook until onion is soft, about 3 minutes.

2. Place celery mixture and all remaining ingredients in large bowl; toss lightly until mixed.

3. Stuff in poultry, as desired, or bake separately (see Chicken Preparation Tips).

Wild Rice Stuffing

Makes about 4 cups (1 L)

⅓ cup (80 mL) butter or margarine
1 cup (250 mL) sliced fresh mushrooms
¾ cup (180 mL) chopped celery
¼ cup (60 mL) finely chopped onion
3 cups (750 mL) cooked wild rice
½ teaspoon (2 mL) salt
¼ teaspoon (1 mL) pepper
¼ teaspoon (1 mL) dried thyme leaves

For that special occasion, wild rice and fresh mushroom stuffing is delicious with any roasted poultry.

1. Melt butter in large skillet over medium heat; add mushrooms, celery and onion. Cook until onion is soft, about 3 minutes.

2. Add remaining ingredients to mushroom mixture; toss lightly until mixed.

3. Stuff in poultry, as desired, or bake separately (see Chicken Preparation Tips).

One~Dish Meals

Easy, meal-in-a-single-dish recipes are included
in this chapter. Among the selections are an old-fashioned
Country Chicken Pie, crisp and colorful
Ratatouille Stir-Fry and a contemporary California Casserole.

Peek-A-Boo Chicken

Makes 4 servings

2   large whole chicken breasts, deboned, skinned and split lengthwise into halves
½   teaspoon (2 mL) salt
⅛   teaspoon (0.5 mL) pepper
    Pinch garlic powder
6   teaspoons (30 mL) butter or margarine, at room temperature
4   pieces feta or brick cheese (about 1½ ounces or 45 g each)
4   small potatoes, cut into halves
12   slices (1 inch or 2.5 cm each) celery
8   slices (1 inch or 2.5 cm each) zucchini
8   slices (1 inch or 2.5 cm each) carrot
1   medium onion, cut into quarters
8   Greek or Italian ripe olives
    Paprika, if desired
    Minced fresh parsley, if desired

In this fun meal, buttered boneless chicken breasts are combined with Greek feta cheese and assorted fresh vegetables in individual foil packets. They can be baked in the oven or on an outdoor grill.

1. Heat oven to 375°F (190°C).

2. Sprinkle chicken lightly with salt, pepper and garlic powder.

3. Cut 4 squares (12 inches or 30 cm each) of aluminum foil. Place one breast half on center of each foil square; spread each chicken piece with 1½ teaspoons (7 mL) of the butter.

4. Place 1 piece cheese on top of each chicken piece; add 2 halves potato, 3 slices celery, 2 slices zucchini, 2 slices carrot, 1 onion quarter and 2 olives.

5. Wrap aluminum foil securely around chicken, cheese and vegetables; place foil packets on large cookie sheet. Bake until chicken is tender, about 45 minutes.*

6. Remove food from foil before serving; sprinkle with paprika and parsley.

*Note: Foil packets can be placed over hot coals and grilled until chicken is tender, 1 to 1¼ hours. Use heavy-duty aluminum foil for wrapping the packets.

Ratatouille Stir-Fry

In this fast and easy dish, chicken and vegetables are stir-fried in a delicate soy- and ginger-flavored sauce.

2   large whole chicken breasts, deboned, skinned and split lengthwise into halves

1   tablespoon (15 mL) vegetable oil

2   cups (500 mL) diagonally sliced celery

1   cup (250 mL) fresh or thawed frozen cut green beans

1   small onion, thinly sliced

½   cup (125 mL) sliced carrot

¼   cup (60 mL) chicken broth

2   medium zucchini, cut into 1x¼-inch (2.5x0.5 cm) strips

1   cup (250 mL) raw cauliflowerettes

½   cup (125 mL) chopped green pepper

⅓   cup (80 mL) soy sauce

½   teaspoon (2 mL) sugar

⅛   teaspoon (0.5 mL) ground ginger

⅛   teaspoon (0.5 mL) ground pepper

⅛   teaspoon (0.5 mL) garlic powder

3   cups (750 mL) torn fresh spinach leaves

1   tablespoon (15 mL) water

2   teaspoons (10 mL) cornstarch

Hot cooked rice or Chinese noodles

1. Cut chicken into 2x¼-inch (5x0.5 cm) strips.

2. Heat oil in wok or large skillet over medium-high heat 1 minute; add chicken, celery, beans, onion and carrot. Cook, stirring frequently, about 3 minutes.

3. Add broth to chicken mixture; cover and cook 3 minutes longer.

4. Add zucchini, cauliflowerettes, green pepper, soy sauce, sugar, ginger, ground pepper and garlic powder to chicken mixture; cook 3 minutes longer. Stir spinach into chicken mixture; cook 2 minutes longer.

5. Blend water and cornstarch in small bowl; stir into chicken mixture. Cook and stir until liquid is thick, 1 to 2 minutes.

6. Serve hot over rice.

Country Chicken Pie

Dilly Pastry (recipe
   follows)
1½ cups (375 mL) sliced carrots
½ cup (125 mL) chopped
   onion
½ cup (125 mL) chopped
   celery
⅓ cup (80 mL) finely chopped
   green pepper
⅓ cup (80 mL) water
¼ cup (60 mL) chicken fat,
   butter or margarine
¼ cup (60 mL) all-purpose
   flour
1 cup (250 mL) chicken broth
1 cup (250 mL) milk
2 cups (500 mL) diced
   cooked chicken
1 package (10 ounces or
   285 g) frozen peas,
   thawed and drained
1 teaspoon (5 mL) salt
Pinch ground pepper

This creamy chicken-vegetable casserole is covered with a blanket of dill-scented pastry and baked until the pastry is flaky and golden.

1. Prepare Dilly Pastry.

2. Heat oven to 400°F (200°C).

3. Place carrots, onion, celery, green pepper and water in 1½-quart (1.5 L) saucepan; cover and cook over medium-high heat about 3 minutes.

4. Melt chicken fat in 2-quart (2 L) saucepan over medium heat; blend in flour. Gradually add broth and milk to flour mixture; cook, stirring constantly, until mixture is thick, about 5 minutes.

5. Reduce heat to low; add chicken, peas, salt and ground pepper. Cook until hot throughout, about 2 minutes. Pour chicken mixture into greased 8-inch (20 cm) square baking dish.

6. Roll pastry on lightly floured surface into a 7-inch (18 cm) square. Cut pastry into 4 squares and place on top of chicken mixture. Bake until pastry is golden, 25 to 30 minutes. Serve hot.

Dilly Pastry

Makes 4 servings

¾ cup (180 mL) all-purpose
   flour
½ teaspoon (2 mL) dried dill
   weed
¼ teaspoon (1 mL) salt
¼ cup (60 mL) shortening
2 to 3 tablespoons (30 to
   45 mL) cold water

1. Mix flour, dill and salt in small bowl; cut in shortening until pieces are size of small peas.

2. Sprinkle 2 tablespoons (30 mL) of the water over flour mixture; mix with fork just until flour is moistened. Add remaining 1 tablespoon (15 mL) water if necessary to form a stiff dough. Shape dough into ball. Cover and refrigerate at least 1 hour or overnight before rolling.

ONE-DISH MEALS

Biscuit-Topped Chicken Casserole

Makes 4 servings

1   can (10¾ ounces or 305 g) condensed cream of chicken soup

1½ cups (375 mL) milk

2   cups (500 mL) cubed cooked chicken

1   package (10 ounces or 285 g) frozen chopped spinach, cooked and drained

¾   cup (180 mL) ricotta cheese

½   cup (125 mL) chopped celery

¼   cup (60 mL) chopped carrot

2   tablespoons (30 mL) grated Parmesan cheese

2   tablespoons (30 mL) finely chopped onion

1   tablespoon (15 mL) minced fresh parsley

1   teaspoon (5 mL) salt

⅛   teaspoon (0.5 mL) pepper

1½ cups (375 mL) all-purpose flour

2   teaspoons (10 mL) baking powder

¼   teaspoon (1 mL) ground sage

⅓   cup (80 mL) shortening

1   egg, lightly beaten

Full of old-fashioned appeal, this chicken, vegetable and cheese dish is covered with a simple biscuit topping. The casserole is perfect for casual family dining.

1. Heat oven to 350°F (180°C).

2. Mix soup and ½ cup (125 mL) of the milk in large mixing bowl until blended; stir in chicken, spinach, ricotta cheese, celery, carrot, Parmesan cheese, onion, parsley, ½ teaspoon (2 mL) of the salt and the pepper.

3. Pour chicken mixture into greased 2-quart (2 L) baking dish.

4. Mix flour, baking powder, remaining ½ teaspoon (2 mL) salt and the sage in medium bowl; cut in shortening until mixture resembles coarse crumbs.

5. Blend egg and remaining 1 cup (250 mL) in milk in small bowl; add to flour mixture, stirring just until flour is moistened.

6. Pour batter over chicken mixture. Bake until biscuit topping is golden, 45 to 55 minutes. Serve hot.

Wild Rice Casserole

Makes 6 servings

12 chicken thighs, deboned and skinned

2½ teaspoons (12 mL) salt

¼   teaspoon (1 mL) pepper

3   tablespoons (45 mL) butter or margarine

1   medium onion, chopped

8   ounces (225 g) fresh mushrooms, sliced
continued

In this sophisticated casserole, wild rice and mushrooms are partially baked in chicken broth and then combined with sautéed chicken thighs.

1. Heat oven to 350°F (180°C).

2. Sprinkle chicken with ½ teaspoon (2 mL) of the salt and ⅛ teaspoon (0.5 mL) of the pepper.

3. Melt the 3 tablespoons (45 mL) butter in large skillet over medium heat; add chicken. Cook until chicken is golden, 4 to 5 minutes on each side. Remove chicken from skillet and reserve.

Wild Rice Casserole *(continued)*

2 teaspoons (10 mL) all-purpose flour
1 cup (250 mL) uncooked wild rice
¼ cup (60 mL) butter or margarine, at room temperature
3 cups (750 mL) hot chicken broth
Spiced apple rings, if desired

4. Add onion and mushrooms to drippings in skillet; cook until onion is soft, about 3 minutes.

5. Add remaining 2 teaspoons (10 mL) salt, remaining ⅛ teaspoon (0.5 mL) pepper and the flour to onion mixture; cook, stirring constantly, until flour is golden, 2 to 3 minutes. Remove from heat.

6. Spread rice evenly over bottom of 13x9x2-inch (33x23x5 cm) baking pan. Combine ¼ cup (60 mL) butter and the hot broth; stir until butter melts. Pour broth mixture over rice; stir in onion mixture. Cover tightly with aluminum foil. Bake 45 minutes.

7. Remove pan from oven; uncover and arrange chicken over rice. Cover tightly. Bake until rice is done and liquid is absorbed, about 45 minutes longer. Garnish with apple rings. Serve hot.

California Casserole

Makes 4 servings

2 large whole chicken breasts, split lengthwise into halves
½ teaspoon (2 mL) salt
¼ teaspoon (1 mL) paprika
⅛ teaspoon (0.5 mL) pepper
2 tablespoons (30 mL) butter or margarine, at room temperature
2 cups (500 mL) raw caulif:lowerettes
2 cups (500 mL) raw broccoli flowerettes
1 cup (250 mL) water
1 can (8 ounces or 225 g) mushroom stems and pieces, drained
1 can (10¾ ounces or 305 g) condensed cream of chicken soup
1 cup (250 mL) plain yogurt, at room temperature
½ cup (125 mL) shredded Cheddar cheese (2 ounces or 60 g)

Yogurt brings out the subtle flavor of cauliflower and broccoli in this attractive dish.

1. Heat oven to 400°F (200°C).

2. Sprinkle chicken with salt, paprika and pepper; rub with butter.

3. Arrange chicken, skin-side up, in greased 13x9x2-inch (33x23x5 cm) baking dish. Bake 20 minutes. Turn chicken over; bake until chicken is almost tender, 10 to 15 minutes longer.

4. While chicken is baking, place cauliflower, broccoli and water in 2-quart (2 L) saucepan; cook over medium heat until vegetables are almost tender, about 10 minutes. Drain vegetables.

5. Remove chicken from oven; arrange chicken in center of the baking dish. Sprinkle cauliflower, broccoli and mushrooms around chicken.

6. Blend soup and yogurt in small bowl; spoon over vegetables. Sprinkle cheese over soup mixture. Bake until hot and bubbly, 15 to 20 minutes longer. Serve hot.

ONE-DISH MEALS

Zucchini Boats

4   large zucchini (about 8 inches or 20 cm long each)
¼   cup (60 mL) butter or margarine
2   tablespoons (30 mL) finely chopped onion
2   cups (500 mL) diced cooked chicken
1½   cups (375 mL) cooked white rice
6   tablespoons (90 mL) tomato sauce
¼   teaspoon (1 mL) plus ⅛ teaspoon (0.5 mL) dried dill weed
¼   teaspoon (1 mL) salt
¼   teaspoon (1 mL) pepper
1½   cups (375 mL) chicken broth

In this interesting meal-in-one dish, hollowed-out zucchini halves are filled with a savory chicken and rice mixture before baking.

1. Heat oven to 350°F (180°C).

2. Cut zucchini lengthwise into halves; scoop out pulp leaving ¼-inch (0.5 cm) edge all around each zucchini. Chop enough pulp to measure ½ cup (125 mL); reserve. (Reserve remaining pulp for another use.)

3. Melt butter in large skillet over medium heat; add ½ cup (125 mL) zucchini pulp and the onion. Cook until zucchini is golden, 3 to 5 minutes.

4. Add chicken, rice, 2 tablespoons (30 mL) of the tomato sauce, ¼ teaspoon (1 mL) of the dill, ⅛ teaspoon (0.5 mL) of the salt and ⅛ teaspoon (0.5 mL) of the pepper to zucchini mixture; cook until hot, 2 to 3 minutes longer. Remove from heat.

5. Spoon chicken mixture into zucchini halves; place zucchini in greased 13x9x2-inch (33x23x5 cm) baking dish. Mix broth, remaining 4 tablespoons (60 mL) tomato sauce, ⅛ teaspoon (0.5 mL) salt, ⅛ teaspoon (0.5 mL) pepper and ⅛ teaspoon (0.5 mL) dill in small bowl.

6. Pour broth mixture around zucchini; cover. Bake 15 minutes. Uncover and bake until zucchini is tender, 15 to 20 minutes longer. Serve hot.

Athenian Baked Chicken

1   broiling/frying chicken (about 3 pounds or 1350 g), cut into serving pieces
1½   tablespoons (22 mL) lemon juice
2   tablespoons (60 mL) olive oil
1   teaspoon (5 mL) salt
1   teaspoon (5 mL) dried oregano leaves
½   teaspoon (2 mL) white pepper
1   can (15 ounces or 425 g) tomato sauce
2   cups (500 mL) hot chicken broth
1   cup (250 mL) hot water
8   ounces (225 g) uncooked curly noodles
     Grated kefalotiri or Parmesan cheese

In Greek fashion, the chicken is rubbed with lemon juice and olive oil and then baked with curly noodles in a piquant tomato sauce made with the pan juices. Freshly grated Greek kefalotiri or Parmesan cheese is served over the noodles to enhance the dish.

1. Heat oven to 400°F (200°C).

2. Rub chicken with lemon juice and olive oil. Arrange chicken, skin-side down, in single layer in greased 13x9x2-inch (33x23x5 cm) baking pan; sprinkle with salt, oregano and pepper. Bake 15 minutes. Turn chicken over; bake 15 minutes longer.

3. Remove pan from oven; place chicken on serving platter. Pour tomato sauce, broth and water into baking pan; loosen pan drippings. Place pan over high heat on top of range; heat to boiling. Place noodles in pan; return to boil, stirring frequently. Remove pan from heat.

4. Arrange chicken pieces over noodles. Bake until noodles and chicken are tender, about 30 minutes longer. Sprinkle with cheese. Serve hot.

Scalloped Chicken and Potatoes

Makes 4 servings

2 tablespoons (30 mL) butter or margarine
2 tablespoons (30 mL) all-purpose flour
1 cup (250 mL) chicken broth
1 cup (250 mL) evaporated milk
1 teaspoon (5 mL) instant minced onion
¾ teaspoon (4 mL) salt
Dash red pepper sauce
2 cups (500 mL) thinly sliced cooked potatoes
2 cups (500 mL) diced cooked chicken
3 tablespoons (45 mL) finely chopped green pepper
2 tablespoons (30 mL) drained chopped pimiento
2 tablespoons (30 mL) dry bread crumbs
1 teaspoon (5 mL) butter or margarine

Bits of pimiento and green pepper add color to this quick and easy creamed chicken and potato casserole.

1. Heat oven to 350°F (180°C).

2. Melt the 2 tablespoons (30 mL) butter in 2-quart (2 L) saucepan over medium heat; blend in flour. Gradually add broth, milk and onion; cook, stirring constantly, until mixture is slightly thick, about 3 minutes. Remove from heat; stir in salt and red pepper sauce. Reserve.

3. Arrange potatoes over bottom of greased 2-quart (2 L) rectangular baking dish. Arrange chicken over potatoes. Sprinkle green pepper and pimiento over chicken. Pour white sauce over all.

4. Place bread crumbs and 1 tablespoon (5 mL) butter in small skillet. Cook over medium heat, stirring constantly, until butter melts and crumbs are coated, 1 to 2 minutes. Sprinkle crumb mixture evenly over casserole. Bake until hot throughout, 20 to 25 minutes. Serve hot.

Stews

When cooked slowly with liquid,
chicken develops a full, rich flavor. On the following pages,
you'll find a variety of taste-tempting dishes,
such as Wine Poached Chicken, Siamese Chicken
and Texas-Style Chicken.

Coq au Vin

Makes 4 to 6 servings

1	broiling/frying chicken (about 3 pounds or 1350 g), cut into serving pieces
5	tablespoons (75 mL) all-purpose flour
¼	cup (60 mL) butter or margarine
¼	cup (60 mL) brandy
1	cup (250 mL) diced cooked ham
8	ounces (225 g) fresh mushrooms, cut into quarters
1	cup (250 mL) dry white or red wine
1	clove garlic, pressed
1	teaspoon (5 mL) salt
1	teaspoon (5 mL) minced fresh parsley
¼	teaspoon (1 mL) pepper
⅛	teaspoon (0.5 mL) dried thyme leaves
1	bay leaf
1	package (20 ounces or 565 g) frozen small whole onions
1	tablespoon (15 mL) water
	Hot cooked rice
	Minced fresh parsley, if desired

Simple to prepare, this classic French dish is perfect for elegant dining.

1. Coat chicken with 4 tablespoons (60 mL) of the flour.

2. Melt butter in large skillet over medium heat; add chicken. Cook until chicken is golden, 7 to 8 minutes on each side.

3. Pour brandy over chicken. Carefully ignite brandy with long wooden match. When flame dies down, cover skillet to extinguish flame.

4. Uncover skillet; add ham, mushrooms, wine, garlic, salt, 1 teaspoon (5 mL) parsley, the pepper, thyme and bay leaf. Reduce heat; cover and simmer 35 minutes.

5. Add onions to skillet; cook until chicken is tender, about 10 minutes longer. Remove bay leaf.

6. Blend remaining 1 tablespoon (15 mL) flour and the water in small bowl; stir into chicken mixture. Cook until liquid is thick, about 5 minutes longer. Serve hot over rice, garnished with remaining parsley.

Savory Ragout

Makes 6 servings

1   broiling/frying chicken (about 3 pounds or 1350 g), cut into serving pieces
1   teaspoon (5 mL) salt
¼   teaspoon (1 mL) pepper
2   tablespoons (30 mL) olive or vegetable oil
2½   cups (625 mL) chicken broth
1   can (8 ounces or 225 g) tomato sauce
1   medium onion, thinly sliced
¼   teaspoon (1 mL) dried summer savory leaves
⅛   teaspoon (0.5 mL) sugar
4   cups (1 L) uncooked medium egg noodles (about 8 ounces or 225 g)
    Grated Parmesan cheese

This is an easy dish to put together when you're short on time. Serve it with a leafy green salad and a crusty loaf of French or Italian bread.

1. Sprinkle chicken with salt and pepper.

2. Heat oil in 5-quart (5 L) Dutch oven over medium heat; add chicken, skin-side down. Cook until chicken is golden, 7 to 8 minutes. Turn chicken over; add broth, tomato sauce, onion, savory and sugar. Cook until broth boils. Reduce heat; cover and cook, stirring occasionally, 30 minutes.

3. Stir noodles into chicken mixture; cook over medium heat until boiling. Cover and cook until noodles are done, about 10 minutes longer.

4. Arrange chicken on serving platter; place noodles around chicken. Sprinkle cheese over all. Serve hot.

Chicken Wings with Okra

Makes 4 servings

8   chicken wings
¾   teaspoon (4 mL) salt
¼   teaspoon (1 mL) pepper
3   tablespoons (45 mL) butter
1   medium onion, chopped
1   clove garlic, pressed
1   can (8 ounces or 225 g) tomato sauce
¼   cup (60 mL) water
¼   teaspoon (1 mL) dried thyme leaves
⅛   teaspoon (0.5 mL) pepper
    Pinch sugar
3   packages (10 ounces or 285 g each) frozen whole okra
1½   tablespoons (22 mL) lemon juice

Okra, the curious little vegetable that finds its way into many famous Creole dishes, is delicious stewed with chicken wings in a piquant tomato sauce.

1. Cut off and discard tip of each wing at first joint; cut apart the two remaining wing parts at the joint. Sprinkle wing parts with ½ teaspoon (2 mL) of the salt and the ¼ teaspoon (1 mL) pepper.

2. Melt butter in 5-quart (5 L) Dutch oven over medium heat; add wing parts. Cook until wings are golden, 7 to 8 minutes on each side. Remove wings from Dutch oven; reserve.

3. Add onion and garlic to drippings in Dutch oven; cook until onion is golden, about 5 minutes.

4. Stir tomato sauce, water, remaining ¼ teaspoon (1 mL) salt, the thyme, ⅛ teaspoon (0.5 mL) pepper and the sugar into onion mixture; heat to boiling.

5. Add okra to tomato mixture; sprinkle with lemon juice. Arrange wing parts over okra. Reduce heat; cover and cook, stirring occasionally, until okra is tender, about 20 minutes. Serve hot.

STEWS

West Indies Chicken

1 broiling/frying chicken (about 3 pounds or 1350 g), cut into serving pieces
1 teaspoon (5 mL) salt
⅛ teaspoon (0.5 mL) cayenne pepper
2 tablespoons (30 mL) butter or margarine
1 tablespoon (15 mL) vegetable oil
½ cup (125 mL) chopped green pepper
¼ cup (60 mL) chopped onion
¼ cup (60 mL) chopped pimiento-stuffed olives
1 clove garlic, minced
1 can (8 ounces or 225 g) tomato sauce
½ cup (125 mL) milk
1 teaspoon (5 mL) minced fresh parsley
¼ teaspoon (1 mL) celery salt
¼ teaspoon (1 mL) sugar
¼ teaspoon (1 mL) dried thyme leaves
½ bay leaf, crushed
   Hot cooked rice

Pimiento-stuffed olives, green pepper and a light tomato sauce add character to this easy stew.

1. Sprinkle chicken with salt and cayenne pepper.

2. Heat butter and oil in large skillet over medium heat; add chicken. Cook until chicken is golden, 7 to 8 minutes.

3. Turn chicken over; add green pepper, onion, olives and garlic. Cook until onion is soft, about 5 minutes.

4. Mix tomato sauce, milk, parsley, celery salt, sugar, thyme and bay leaf; pour over chicken mixture. Reduce heat; cover and cook until chicken is tender, about 40 minutes.

5. Place rice on serving platter; arrange chicken over rice. Spoon tomato mixture over chicken. Serve hot.

Bavarian Stewed Chicken

1 stewing hen (about 5 pounds or 2250 g), cut into serving pieces
   Water
1 stalk celery (including leaves), cut into 2-inch (5 cm) pieces
1 small onion, cut into halves
1 clove garlic, cut into halves
1 bay leaf
2¼ teaspoons (11 mL) salt
   continued

This hearty dish is nice for casual family dinners. It consists of stewed chicken, herb-seasoned mashed potato dumplings and a rich sage-flavored gravy made from chicken broth.

1. Place chicken, giblets and neck in 5-quart (5 L) Dutch oven. Add enough water to reach a level of 1 inch (2.5 cm) above chicken; heat to boiling over high heat. Skim off foam.

2. Add celery, onion, garlic, bay leaf, 2 teaspoons (10 mL) of the salt and the peppercorns to chicken. Reduce heat to low; cover and cook until chicken is tender, 2½ to 3 hours. Remove chicken from Dutch oven, reserving chicken and the broth. Keep chicken warm.

Bavarian Stewed Chicken (continued)

1   teaspoon (5 mL) whole
        peppercorns
     Potato Dumplings (recipe
        follows)
3   tablespoons (45 mL) all-
        purpose flour
⅓   cup (80 mL) cold water
½   teaspoon (2 mL) ground
        sage
⅛   teaspoon (0.5 mL) ground
        pepper
     Paprika

3. Prepare Potato Dumplings.

4. Heat broth in Dutch oven over medium heat to boiling. Drop dumplings carefully into gently boiling broth using slotted spoon. Reduce heat; cover and cook until dumplings are done and float to the top, 10 to 15 minutes. (Do not uncover during cooking.) Remove dumplings from broth; drain on paper toweling. Keep warm.

5. Strain broth through fine sieve. Return 2 cups (500 mL) of the strained broth to the Dutch oven. Reserve remaining broth for another use.

6. Blend flour, ⅓ cup (80 mL) cold water, sage, remaining ¼ teaspoon (1 mL) salt and the ground pepper; gradually stir into broth.

7. Cook over medium heat, stirring constantly, until slightly thick, about 5 minutes. Reduce heat; simmer, stirring frequently, 10 minutes.

8. Arrange chicken and dumplings on serving platter. Pour about ½ cup (125 mL) of the gravy over chicken and dumplings; sprinkle with paprika. Pass remaining gravy.

Makes about 24

Potato Dumplings

1   pound (450 g) potatoes,
        peeled, boiled and
        drained (about
        3 medium)
3   tablespoons (45 mL) butter
        or margarine, melted
1   egg, slightly beaten
6   tablespoons (90 mL) all-
        purpose flour
1½   teaspoons (7 mL) dried
        parsley flakes
½   teaspoon (2 mL) salt
¼   teaspoon (1 mL) ground
        sage
¼   teaspoon (1 mL) dried
        marjoram leaves
⅛   teaspoon (0.5 mL) ground
        nutmeg
⅛   teaspoon (0.5 mL) pepper

1. Mash potatoes with all other ingredients; shape into 1-inch (2.5 cm) balls.

2. Cook as directed in Bavarian Stewed Chicken.

Wine Poached Chicken

Makes 6 servings

1   roasting chicken (about 5 pounds or 2250 g)
1   tablespoon (15 mL) salt
1   teaspoon (5 mL) pepper
2   tablespoons (30 mL) butter or margarine
3   carrots, pared and cut into 1-inch (2.5 cm) pieces
3   stalks celery, cut diagonally into 1-inch (2.5 cm) pieces
4   small whole onions
1   bay leaf
¼   teaspoon (1 mL) dried basil leaves
¼   teaspoon (1 mL) dried oregano leaves
¼   teaspoon (1 mL) dried thyme leaves
1½   cups (375 mL) dry white wine
1   cup (250 mL) chicken broth
    Hot Raisin Glaze (recipe follows)

For the best flavor, select a plump roasting chicken or stewing hen for this recipe. After poaching in herb-seasoned white wine, the tender chicken is served with a hot raisin and cashew glaze.

1. Rub chicken with salt and pepper; tie legs together.

2. Melt butter in 5-quart (5 L) Dutch oven over medium heat; add chicken. Cook until chicken is light brown on all sides, about 10 minutes. Remove chicken from pan; reserve.

3. Place carrots, celery, onions and bay leaf in Dutch oven. Combine basil, oregano and thyme in small bowl; rub evenly over chicken. Place chicken, breast-side down, on top of vegetables in Dutch oven; add wine and broth. Cook over medium heat until liquid boils. Reduce heat to low; cover and simmer 30 minutes.

4. Turn chicken over, breast-side up. Cook until chicken is tender, about 25 minutes longer. Transfer chicken and vegetables to serving platter. Remove strings from legs. Keep chicken warm in 200°F (90°C) oven until ready to serve.

5. Prepare Hot Raisin Glaze. Spoon about ½ cup (125 mL) of the glaze over chicken. Pass remaining glaze with chicken.

Hot Raisin Glaze

Makes 2½ cups (625 mL)

2   tablespoons (30 mL) butter or margarine
⅓   cup (80 mL) all-purpose flour
2   cups (500 mL) chicken broth or strained cooking liquid from Wine Poached Chicken
½   cup (125 mL) golden raisins
⅓   cup (80 mL) chopped cashews
¼   teaspoon (1 mL) salt
⅛   teaspoon (0.5 mL) pepper

1. Melt butter in 2-quart (2 L) saucepan over medium heat; add flour. Cook until flour bubbles.

2. Blend broth gradually into flour mixture. Cook, stirring constantly, until almost thick, 2 to 3 minutes; add raisins, cashews, salt and pepper. Cook until thick, 1 to 2 minutes longer.

Siamese Chicken

Makes 4 to 6 servings

2 cups (500 mL) whipping cream
1½ cups (375 mL) shredded coconut
3 whole chicken breasts, split lengthwise into halves
3 tablespoons (45 mL) ground peanuts
2 green onions, finely chopped
1 clove garlic, minced
1 tablespoon (15 mL) grated lemon rind
1 tablespoon (15 mL) soy sauce
1 teaspoon (5 mL) sugar
½ teaspoon (2 mL) crushed dried red pepper
¼ teaspoon (1 mL) ground coriander
Hot cooked rice

This is a unique and tantalizing way to prepare chicken breasts. They are simmered in a creamy coconut sauce, then served over fluffy hot rice and garnished with toasted coconut.

1. Place cream and coconut in 1½-quart (1.5 L) saucepan; cook over medium heat until boiling. Remove from heat; let stand 30 minutes.

2. Pour cream through sieve, pressing all liquid from coconut. Reserve cream and ½ cup (125 mL) of the coconut. Discard remaining coconut or reserve for another use.

3. Place chicken, skin-side down, in large skillet. Pour reserved cream over chicken; cover and cook over low heat 30 minutes.

4. Mix peanuts, onion, garlic, lemon rind, soy sauce, sugar, red pepper and coriander in small bowl; stir into chicken mixture.

5. Turn chicken breasts skin-side up; cover and simmer until chicken is tender, about 15 minutes longer. Spoon cream mixture over breasts several times during cooking.

6. Meanwhile, heat oven to 350°F (180°C). Sprinkle coconut over greased cookie sheet. Bake until coconut is golden, about 5 minutes.

7. Arrange chicken over rice on serving platter. Pour cream mixture over chicken; sprinkle with toasted coconut. Serve hot.

Chicken Italiano

Makes 4 servings

2 cups (500 mL) Tomato-Herb Sauce (see Index for page number)
4 whole chicken breasts, split lengthwise into halves
2 tablespoons (30 mL) lemon juice
1 teaspoon (5 mL) salt
½ teaspoon (2 mL) dried oregano leaves
⅛ teaspoon (0.5 mL) pepper
2 tablespoons (30 mL) olive oil
1 tablespoon (15 mL) butter
12 ounces (340 g) thin spaghetti
Grated Parmesan cheese

This easy main dish is as good for entertaining as it is for casual family dinners. To complete the meal, add a leafy green salad, a loaf of hot, crusty Italian bread and a bottle of Chianti.

1. Prepare Tomato-Herb Sauce.

2. Sprinkle chicken with lemon juice, salt, oregano and pepper.

3. Heat oil and butter in large skillet over medium heat; add chicken, skin-side down. Cover and cook until chicken is golden, about 10 minutes. Turn chicken over; cover and cook about 5 minutes longer.

4. Pour Tomato-Herb Sauce over chicken. Reduce heat; cover and cook until chicken is tender, about 30 minutes. Stir once during cooking.

5. Cook spaghetti according to package directions until tender; drain. Place spaghetti on large serving platter; top with chicken. Pour sauce over all; sprinkle with cheese. Serve hot.

STEWS

Chicken Skillet Supper

Makes 4 to 6 servings

1½ teaspoons (7 mL) salt
¼ teaspoon (1 mL) pepper
¼ teaspoon (1 mL) ground paprika
⅛ teaspoon (0.5 mL) garlic powder
1 broiling/frying chicken (about 3 pounds or 1350 g), cut into serving pieces
1 tablespoon (15 mL) vegetable oil
2 tablespoons (30 mL) water
1 medium onion, chopped
1 medium potato, pared and cut into 2x¼-inch (5x0.5 cm) French fry-style strips
1 tablespoon (15 mL) slivered almonds, if desired
1 can (8 ounces or 225 g) tomato sauce
1 cup (250 mL) chicken broth
1 teaspoon (5 mL) sugar
1 package (10 ounces or 285 g) frozen French-style green beans or mixed vegetables

Simple and delicious, this chicken and vegetable stew can be prepared in less than one hour.

1. Mix salt, pepper, paprika and garlic powder in small bowl; rub over chicken.

2. Heat oil in large skillet over medium heat; add chicken, skin-side down. Cover and cook 10 minutes. Add water to chicken; cover and cook 30 minutes longer, turning chicken over every 10 minutes. Remove chicken from skillet; reserve.

3. Add onion, potato and almonds to drippings in skillet; cook until onion is soft, about 3 minutes.

4. Add tomato sauce, broth and sugar to onion mixture; cook until liquid boils.

5. Add beans and chicken pieces to tomato mixture; cover and cook until beans are done, about 10 minutes. Serve hot.

Texas-Style Chicken

Makes 4 servings

1 broiling/frying chicken (about 3 pounds or 1350 g), cut into serving pieces
1 teaspoon (5 mL) salt
¼ teaspoon (1 mL) pepper
⅓ cup (80 mL) all-purpose flour
¼ cup (60 mL) olive or vegetable oil *continued*

Easy-to-prepare for entertaining, chicken pieces are simmered with tomatoes, onion and green pepper in this hearty dish. To complete the meal in Texas-style fashion, serve it with fluffy mashed potatoes and buttered corn-on-the cob.

1. Sprinkle chicken with salt and pepper; dip chicken in flour, pressing firmly to coat. Shake off excess flour.

2. Heat oil in large skillet over medium heat; add chicken, skin-side down. Cook until chicken is golden, 7 to 8 minutes on each side. Remove chicken; reserve.

Texas-Style Chicken *(continued)*

2 green peppers, cut into
  ¼-inch (0.5 cm) wide
  strips
1 large onion, sliced
  lengthwise
1 clove garlic, crushed
1 teaspoon (5 mL) salt
1 teaspoon (5 mL) dried
  thyme leaves
⅛ teaspoon (0.5 mL) ground
  pepper
1 can (14½ ounces or 415 g)
  stewed tomatoes

3. Add green pepper, onion, garlic, salt, thyme and ground pepper to oil in skillet; cook until onion is soft, about 5 minutes.

4. Add tomatoes to green pepper mixture; heat to boiling. Return chicken to skillet. Reduce heat; cover and cook until chicken is tender, about 35 minutes longer. Serve hot.

Makes 4 servings

Cinnamon Chicken

1 broiling/frying chicken
  (about 3 pounds or
  1350 g), cut into serving
  pieces
1 teaspoon (5 mL) salt
¼ teaspoon (1 mL) pepper
2 tablespoons (30 mL)
  vegetable oil
¼ cup (60 mL) chopped onion
¼ cup (60 mL) chopped
  celery
1 cup (250 mL) uncooked rice
2 cups (500 mL) chicken
  broth
1 can (8 ounces or 225 g)
  tomato sauce
1 teaspoon (5 mL) lemon
  juice
½ teaspoon (2 mL) sugar
¼ to ½ teaspoon (1 to 2 mL)
  ground cinnamon
1 can (14 ounces or 400 g),
  drained, or 1 package
  (10 ounces or 285 g)
  frozen artichoke hearts,
  thawed*

This easy main dish features chicken, rice and artichoke hearts stewed in a light, cinnamon-spiced tomato sauce.

1. Cut chicken breast in half lengthwise; cut each crosswise in half again. Sprinkle chicken with ½ teaspoon (2 mL) of the salt and ⅛ teaspoon (0.5 mL) of the pepper.

2. Heat oil in 5-quart (5 L) Dutch oven over medium heat; add chicken, skin-side down. Cover and cook 15 minutes. Turn chicken over; cook 15 minutes longer. Remove chicken from pan; reserve.

3. Cook onion and celery in Dutch oven until onion is soft, about 5 minutes; add rice. Cook 1 minute longer.

4. Add broth, tomato sauce, lemon juice, remaining ½ teaspoon (2 mL) salt, the sugar, cinnamon and remaining ⅛ teaspoon (0.5 mL) pepper to the rice mixture; heat to boiling. Reduce heat; cover and simmer 10 minutes.

5. Cut artichokes into quarters. Arrange chicken and artichokes over rice mixture. Cover and cook until rice is done, 15 to 20 minutes longer.

6. Arrange chicken in center of serving platter. Spoon rice and artichokes around chicken. Serve hot.

*Note: 1 can (15 ounces or 425 g) drained garbanzo beans or chick-peas can be substituted for the artichokes.

Chicken Marengo

The first version of this dish reportedly was served to Napoleon Bonaparte following his victory over the Austrians in Marengo, Italy in 1800. He loved it, and so will you!

1	broiling/frying chicken (about 3 pounds or 1350 g), cut into serving pieces
1	teaspoon (5 mL) salt
¼	teaspoon (1 mL) pepper
2	tablespoons (30 mL) olive oil
2	tablespoons (30 mL) butter or margarine
¼	cup (60 mL) finely chopped onion
1	small clove garlic, pressed
1	can (16 ounces or 450 g) undrained Italian-style tomatoes, cut up
½	cup (125 mL) chicken broth
⅓	cup (80 mL) Madeira wine
½	teaspoon (2 mL) dried thyme leaves
8	ounces (225 g) cooked shrimp
12	pitted ripe olives
8	large mushrooms, sliced Vegetable oil
4	Small eggs*
4	slices bread, cut diagonally into halves and toasted*

1. Sprinkle chicken with salt and pepper.

2. Heat olive oil and 1 tablespoon (15 mL) of the butter in 5-quart (5 L) Dutch oven over medium heat; add chicken, skin-side down. Cook until chicken is golden, 7 to 8 minutes. Turn chicken over; add onion and garlic. Cook until onion is soft, about 3 minutes.

3. Add tomatoes, broth, Madeira and thyme to chicken mixture. Reduce heat; cover and simmer until chicken is tender, about 40 minutes.

4. Remove chicken from Dutch oven; reserve.

5. Pour the cooking mixture from the chicken into food processor or blender container; process until vegetables are pureed. Return mixture to Dutch oven.

6. Add chicken, shrimp and olives to vegetable mixture; cover and cook over medium heat until hot. Keep warm.

7. Melt remaining 1 tablespoon (15 mL) butter in small skillet over medium heat; add mushrooms. Cook, stirring frequently, until mushrooms are golden, about 5 minutes; reserve.

8. Pour vegetable oil into 1½-quart (1.5 L) saucepan until it reaches a level of ½ inch (1.5 cm); heat over medium heat to 350°F (180°C). Break 1 egg into saucer or small custard cup; slide egg carefully into hot oil. Shape egg white into round ball by gently rolling it against side of pan using wooden spoon; cook until yolk is almost set, 1 to 2 minutes. Turn egg over; cook until yolk is set, about 1 minute longer. Remove egg from oil with slotted spoon and drain on paper toweling. Repeat to cook remaining 3 eggs.

9. Place chicken in center of large serving platter; arrange toast around chicken. Place eggs on top of every other piece of toast. Sprinkle mushrooms over chicken. Pour vegetable mixture over chicken. Serve hot.

*Note: Hot cooked rice can be substituted for the eggs and toast points.

Martha's Chicken

1	broiling/frying chicken (about 3 pounds or 1350 g), cut into serving pieces
1	tablespoon (15 mL) lemon juice
1	teaspoon (5 mL) salt
1/8	teaspoon (0.5 mL) pepper
1/3	cup (80 mL) all-purpose flour
2	tablespoons (30 mL) olive oil
2	tablespoons (30 mL) butter or margarine
1/4	cup (60 mL) chopped onion
2	cups (500 mL) chicken broth
1	cup (250 mL) water
1	can (6 ounces or 170 g) tomato paste
8	whole cloves
2	sticks cinnamon (2 inches or 5 cm long each), cut crosswise into halves
1	large clove garlic, cut into halves
1	whole orange, cut into halves
	Cheese Macaroni (recipe follows), if desired

A spicy bouquet of cloves, cinnamon and garlic, plus a fresh orange accent, make this chicken dish outstanding. It is especially good when served over macaroni that has been tossed with grated Parmesan cheese.

1. Sprinkle chicken with lemon juice, salt and pepper. Coat chicken with flour.

2. Heat oil and butter in 5-quart (5 L) Dutch oven over medium heat; add chicken, skin-side down. Cook until chicken is golden, 7 to 8 minutes. Turn chicken over and cook 5 minutes; add onion. Cook 5 minutes longer.

3. Blend broth, water and tomato paste in medium bowl; pour over chicken.

4. Tie cloves, cinnamon and garlic in 4-inch (10 cm) square of cheesecloth; add to chicken mixture.

5. Squeeze juice from orange halves and pour over chicken mixture. Place orange halves in Dutch oven with chicken. Cook over medium heat until liquid boils. Reduce heat; cover and simmer until chicken is tender, about 35 minutes.

6. Meanwhile, prepare Cheese Macaroni. When chicken is done, place macaroni in center of serving platter. Arrange chicken around macaroni.

7. Remove and discard spice bag and orange halves from tomato mixture. Pour tomato mixture over chicken and macaroni. Serve hot.

Cheese Macaroni

1	package (8 ounces or 225 g) thick long macaroni or mostaccioli
3	tablespoons (45 mL) butter or margarine, melted
1/3	cup (80 mL) grated Parmesan cheese

1. Cook macaroni according to package directions; drain.

2. Toss macaroni lightly with butter until coated; add cheese. Toss until macaroni is coated. Keep warm.

Makes 4 servings

Broccoli Chicken

1½ pounds (675 g) fresh
    broccoli
3   cups (750 mL) water
1   broiling/frying chicken
    (about 3 pounds or
    1350 g), cut into serving
    pieces
1½ tablespoons (22 mL) lemon
    juice
1   teaspoon (5 mL) salt
⅛   teaspoon (0.5 mL) pepper
¼   cup (60 mL) butter or
    margarine
1   medium onion, finely
    chopped
1   tablespoon (15 mL) flour
1   tablespoon (15 mL) water
½   cup (125 mL) half and half
    Lemon slices, if desired

Broccoli adds distinctive flavor and bright color to this chicken main dish. Part of the broccoli is pureed and stirred into the dish during the last few minutes of cooking; the remainder is served in stalks around the chicken.

1. Place ¼ pound (115 g) of the broccoli and 1 cup (250 mL) of the water in 1-quart (1 L) saucepan; cook over medium heat until broccoli is tender, about 15 minutes. Drain, reserving broccoli and cooking liquid. Place cooked broccoli and 2 tablespoons (30 mL) of the cooking liquid in food processor or blender container; process until pureed. Reserve.

2. Sprinkle chicken with lemon juice, salt and pepper.

3. Melt butter in large skillet over medium heat; add chicken, skin-side down. Cook until chicken is golden, 7 to 8 minutes. Turn chicken over. Add onions to chicken; cook 5 minutes longer.

4. Add remaining reserved broccoli liquid to chicken. Reduce heat; cover and cook until chicken is tender, about 30 minutes.

5. While chicken is cooking, cut remaining 1¼ pounds (565 g) broccoli into serving-size stalks. Place broccoli and remaining 2 cups (500 mL) water in 5-quart (5 L) Dutch oven. Cover and cook over low heat until broccoli is tender, 15 to 20 minutes. Remove from heat; keep warm.

6. Mix flour and 1 tablespoon (15 mL) water in small bowl; stir into chicken mixture. Stir half and half and pureed broccoli into chicken mixture; cook, stirring constantly, until sauce is thick, about 5 to 8 minutes longer.

7. Place chicken in center of large serving platter. Drain broccoli and arrange around chicken. Spoon sauce over all. Serve hot, garnished with lemon slices.

Sauces

Sauces complement a variety of
chicken dishes. Madeira, Bordelaise, cheese, curry,
creole, or barbecue sauce—any of these
can add just the right touch to your favorite
chicken recipes.

Louisiana Creole Sauce

Makes 2 cups (500 mL)

2 tablespoons (30 mL) vegetable oil
½ cup (125 mL) chopped onion
¼ cup (60 mL) chopped celery
¼ cup (60 mL) chopped green pepper
2 tablespoons (30 mL) chopped pimiento-stuffed olives
1 clove garlic, minced
1 cup (250 mL) chopped canned tomatoes
¾ cup (180 mL) chicken broth
½ cup (125 mL) tomato paste
½ teaspoon (2 mL) salt
¼ teaspoon (1 mL) sugar
¼ teaspoon (1 mL) dried thyme leaves
⅛ teaspoon (0.5 mL) cayenne pepper
⅛ teaspoon (0.5 mL) red pepper sauce
½ small bay leaf

Good served over fried or roasted chicken, this is a somewhat peppery sauce for those who like an emphatic accent to their food. Those who are less adventuresome might wish to cut down on the amount of cayenne and red pepper sauce.

1. Heat oil in 2-quart (2 L) saucepan over medium heat; add onion, celery, green pepper, olives and garlic. Cook until onion is golden, about 5 minutes.

2. Add remaining ingredients to onion mixture; cook, stirring occasionally, until mixture boils.

3. Reduce heat; cover and simmer until sauce is slightly thick, about 10 minutes. Remove bay leaf before serving. Serve hot.

SAUCES

Swiss Cheese Sauce

Makes 1½ cups (375 mL)

2 tablespoons (30 mL) butter
2 tablespoons (30 mL) all-purpose flour
1¼ cups (310 mL) milk
½ cup (125 mL) shredded Swiss cheese (2 ounces or 60 g)
¼ teaspoon (1 mL) salt
Dash white pepper
2 tablespoons (30 mL) chopped green pepper
1 tablespoon (15 mL) drained chopped pimiento

Green pepper and pimiento add color and flavor to this delicate cheese-flavored white sauce.

1. Melt butter in 1-quart (1 L) saucepan; stir in flour. Cook over low heat, stirring constantly, until bubbly, 1 to 2 minutes.

2. Stir milk into flour mixture. Cook, stirring constantly, until sauce is thick, about 5 minutes. Remove from heat.

3. Add cheese, salt and white pepper to sauce; stir until cheese melts. Stir green pepper and pimiento into sauce. Cook and stir over low heat until hot throughout, 1 to 2 minutes longer. Serve hot.

Pacific Barbecue Sauce

Makes about 2⅓ cups (580 mL)

1 cup (250 mL) soy sauce
¾ cup (180 mL) chili sauce
½ cup (125 mL) orange marmalade
2 tablespoons (30 mL) honey
½ teaspoon (2 mL) ground ginger

Charcoal-grilled chicken is savory and moist when marinated and basted with this fruity, soy sauce mixture.

1. Mix all ingredients in small bowl. (Sauce can be stored covered in refrigerator up to 2 weeks.)

Sauce Divine

Makes about ¾ cup (180 mL)

4 egg yolks
1 tablespoon (15 mL) cold water
½ cup (125 mL) butter, melted
1 teaspoon (5 mL) fresh lemon juice
3 tablespoons (45 mL) half and half
2 tablespoons (30 mL) dry sherry
¼ teaspoon (1 mL) salt
Pinch white pepper

Similar to Hollandaise, this rich, creamy egg yolk and butter sauce is laced with a touch of sherry. It is an excellent accompaniment to hot or cold chicken breast meat.

1. Place egg yolks and water in heavy 1-quart (1 L) saucepan; cook over low heat beating with a whisk until mixture forms thick custard, 2 to 3 minutes.

2. Slowly drizzle butter into yolk mixture, beating constantly.

3. Blend remaining ingredients into yolk mixture; cook, stirring constantly, just until hot. Remove from heat. Serve immediately.

Tarragon-Yogurt Sauce

Makes about 1½ cups (375 mL)

1 cup (250 mL) plain yogurt
½ cup (125 mL) mayonnaise
2 tablespoons (30 mL) minced fresh chives
1½ tablespoons (22 mL) minced fresh or 1½ teaspoons (7 mL) dried tarragon or basil leaves
¼ teaspoon (1 mL) salt
⅛ teaspoon (0.5 mL) garlic powder
⅛ teaspoon (0.5 mL) pepper

This versatile sauce can be used as an accompaniment for chilled cooked poultry slices or as a dressing to pour over a cold poultry and mixed green salad.

1. Blend all ingredients in small bowl. Cover and refrigerate at least 1 hour to blend flavors. (Sauce can be stored covered in refrigerator up to 1 week.)

Sweet-Sour Barbecue Sauce

Makes about 1½ cups (375 mL)

1½ teaspoons (7 mL) cornstarch
8 tablespoons (125 mL) water
1 can (6 ounces or 170 g) tomato paste
2 tablespoons (30 mL) brown sugar
2 tablespoons (30 mL) chili sauce
2 tablespoons (30 mL) vegetable oil
1 tablespoon (15 mL) plus 2 teaspoons (10 mL) vinegar
2 teaspoons (10 mL) instant minced onion
1 teaspoon (5 mL) salt
½ teaspoon (2 mL) Worcestershire sauce
¼ teaspoon (1 mL) celery salt
¼ teaspoon (1 mL) garlic powder
¼ teaspoon (1 mL) lemon pepper
¼ teaspoon (1 mL) ground pepper
⅛ teaspoon (0.5 mL) red pepper sauce

This robust sauce is excellent for use as a basting marinade for barbecued chicken.

1. Blend cornstarch and 1 tablespoon (15 mL) of the water in 1-quart (1 L) saucepan; blend in remaining ingredients.

2. Cook over medium-high heat until mixture boils. Reduce heat and simmer 5 to 7 minutes.

SAUCES

Bordelaise Sauce

Makes 4 cups (1 L)

8 tablespoons (125 mL) butter or margarine
½ cup (125 mL) finely chopped onion
¼ cup (60 mL) finely chopped celery
¼ cup (60 mL) finely chopped carrot
6 tablespoons (90 mL) all-purpose flour
1 quart (1 L) chicken broth
½ cup (125 mL) Bordeaux or other dry red wine
2 tablespoons (30 mL) tomato paste
1 large bay leaf
2½ teaspoons (12 mL) salt
½ teaspoon (2 mL) sugar
¼ teaspoon (1 mL) pepper

The vegetables in this sauce are sautéed, simmered and then pressed through a sieve to extract their precious juices.

1. Melt 6 tablespoons (90 mL) of the butter in a 2-quart (2 L) saucepan over medium heat; add onion, celery and carrot. Cook until onion is golden, about 5 minutes.

2. Stir flour into onion mixture; cook, stirring constantly, 3 minutes longer.

3. Stir remaining ingredients into flour mixture; cook, stirring constantly, until sauce is slightly thick, about 5 minutes. Reduce heat; cook, stirring occasionally, 20 minutes.

4. Strain sauce; press vegetables through sieve. Return sauce to pan.

5. Stir remaining 2 tablespoons (30 mL) butter into sauce; cook over medium heat until butter melts. Serve hot. (Sauce can be prepared in advance, covered and refrigerated for several days; reheat before serving.)

Champignon Sauce

Makes about 2½ cups (625 mL)

2 cups (500 mL) sliced fresh mushrooms
¼ cup (60 mL) dry white wine
1 tablespoon (15 mL) brandy
¼ cup (60 mL) butter or margarine
¼ cup (60 mL) all-purpose flour
1 cup (250 mL) chicken broth
1 cup (250 mL) milk
½ teaspoon (2 mL) salt
⅛ teaspoon (0.5 mL) white pepper
½ teaspoon (2 mL) sugar
2 egg yolks
2 tablespoons (30 mL) whipping cream

In this elegant white sauce, mushrooms are simmered in wine then set aflame with brandy. The velvety sauce is delicious served over sautéed chicken breasts.

1. Cook mushrooms and wine in small saucepan over medium heat until all liquid evaporates; add brandy and carefully ignite using long wooden match. Reserve.

2. Melt butter in 1-quart (1 L) saucepan; stir in flour. Cook over low heat, stirring constantly, until mixture is bubbly, 1 to 2 minutes. Stir broth and milk into flour mixture. Cook, stirring constantly, until sauce is thick, about 5 minutes. Stir salt, pepper and sugar into sauce.

3. Beat egg yolks and cream in small bowl with whisk or fork. Stir about ½ cup (125 mL) of the hot sauce into egg yolk mixture. Blend egg yolk mixture slowly into hot sauce in saucepan; stir in mushrooms. Cook over low heat until hot but not boiling. Serve hot.

Madeira Sauce

Makes 1¼ cups (375 mL)

2 tablespoons (30 mL) butter or margarine
¼ cup (60 mL) finely chopped onion
¼ cup (60 mL) finely chopped celery
1 tablespoon (15 mL) minced ham
1 clove garlic, pressed
1 tablespoon (15 mL) all-purpose flour
1 cup (250 mL) chicken broth
1 teaspoon (5 mL) minced fresh parsley
1 teaspoon (5 mL) tomato paste
¼ teaspoon (1 mL) salt
¼ teaspoon (1 mL) dried thyme leaves
⅛ teaspoon (0.5 mL) pepper
½ cup (125 mL) Madeira wine

This elegant wine sauce, which captures all of the rich flavor and bouquet of the Madeira grapes, is delicious served with a variety of poultry dishes including roasted chicken. For convenience, it can be prepared in advance, refrigerated, then reheated just before serving.

1. Melt butter in 1-quart (1 L) saucepan over medium heat; add onion, celery, ham and garlic. Cook until onion is golden, about 3 minutes.

2. Stir flour into onion mixture; cook, stirring constantly, until flour is golden, 2 to 3 minutes. Add broth, parsley, tomato paste, salt, thyme, and pepper to flour mixture. Reduce heat; cover and simmer 10 minutes.

3. Cook wine in small saucepan over high heat until it is reduced to about 3 tablespoons (45 mL). Stir wine into broth mixture. Cook 2 minutes longer.

4. Strain sauce through sieve using rubber spatula to press liquid out of vegetables. Serve hot. (Sauce can be prepared in advance, covered and refrigerated for several days; reheat before serving.)

Tomato-Herb Sauce

Makes about 4 cups (1 L)

1 can (15 ounces or 425 g) tomato sauce
1 can (6 ounces or 170 g) tomato paste
¾ cup (180 mL) water
1 large clove garlic, pressed
2 tablespoons (30 mL) grated Parmesan cheese
2 teaspoons (10 mL) minced fresh parsley
1½ teaspoons (7 mL) dried oregano leaves
1 teaspoon (5 mL) salt
¾ teaspoon (4 mL) dried basil leaves
½ teaspoon (2 mL) sugar
¼ teaspoon (1 mL) pepper
1 bay leaf

This flavorful sauce simmers to thick richness and is excellent for recipes such as Chicken Italiano (see Index for page number).

1. Mix all ingredients in 2-quart (2 L) saucepan; cook over medium heat until mixture boils.

2. Reduce heat; cook, stirring occasionally, until sauce is slightly thick, 5 to 10 minutes. Remove bay leaf. (Sauce can be refrigerated covered up to 5 days or frozen in a plastic container several months.)

SAUCES

Herbed Mayonnaise

Makes about 1 cup (250 mL)

1 cup (250 mL) mayonnaise
2 tablespoons (30 mL)
     minced fresh parsley
2 tablespoons (30 mL)
     minced fresh chives
2 teaspoons (10 mL)
     prepared mustard
1 small clove garlic, pressed
¼ teaspoon (1 mL) salt
⅛ teaspoon (0.5 mL) pepper

It takes little time or effort to add zest to commercially prepared mayonnaise. Vary the flavor by adding your own favorite herbs, and use the mayonnaise as a spread for cold chicken sandwiches or as a dressing base for chicken salads and appetizers.

1. Blend all ingredients in small bowl. Cover and refrigerate at least 1 hour to blend flavors. (Mayonnaise can be stored covered in refrigerator up to 2 weeks.)

Velouté Sauce

Makes 2 cups (500 mL)

3 tablespoons (45 mL)
     butter or margarine
¼ cup (60 mL) all-purpose
     flour
2 cups (500 mL) chicken
     broth
½ teaspoon (2 mL) salt
¼ teaspoon (1 mL) sugar
⅛ teaspoon (0.5 mL) white
     pepper
2 egg yolks
2 tablespoons (30 mL)
     whipping cream

This is a basic Béchamel or white sauce made with chicken stock instead of milk. Its creamy, velvety texture makes it perfect for serving with sautéed chicken breasts.

1. Melt butter in 1-quart (1 L) saucepan over medium heat; stir in flour to make smooth paste. Cook 1 minute.

2. Blend broth gradually into flour mixture. Cook, stirring constantly, until sauce is thick, about 5 minutes. Stir salt, sugar and pepper into sauce.

3. Blend egg yolks and cream in small bowl; stir about ½ cup (125 mL) of the hot sauce into yolk mixture.

4. Blend yolk mixture slowly into hot sauce in saucepan. Cook over low heat just until hot but not boiling. Serve immediately.

Raisin Sauce

Makes about 1½ cups (375 mL)

1 cup (250 mL) apple juice
1 tablespoon (15 mL)
     cornstarch
2 tablespoons (30 mL) butter
     or margarine
½ cup (125 mL) golden raisins
     Pinch salt

This fruity apple-raisin sauce accents either broiled or roasted poultry.

1. Blend apple juice and cornstarch in 1-quart (1 L) saucepan; add butter. Cook over medium heat until mixture boils. Cook stirring constantly, until sauce is thick, 1 to 2 minutes.

2. Remove sauce from heat; stir in raisins and salt. Serve hot.

Curry Sauce

Makes 1¼ cups (310 mL)

4   teaspoons (20 mL) cornstarch
1   cup (250 mL) water
2   tablespoons (30 mL) butter or margarine
1   teaspoon (5 mL) instant chicken bouillon granules
¼   teaspoon (1 mL) salt
    Pinch pepper
¼   cup (60 mL) half and half or milk
¼   to ½ teaspoon (1 to 2 mL) curry powder

Fast to prepare, this exotically-spiced sauce lends a fabulous flavor to roasted or fried chicken.

1. Combine cornstarch and water in 1-quart (1 L) saucepan; mix well. Add butter, bouillon, salt and pepper to cornstarch mixture.

2. Cook over medium heat, stirring occasionally, until mixture boils; boil 1 minute. Reduce heat; stir in half and half and curry. Cook just until hot but not boiling. Serve hot.

Horseradish Sauce

Makes about ¾ cup (180 mL)

⅓   cup (80 mL) plain yogurt
⅓   cup (80 mL) mayonnaise
2   tablespoons (30 mL) drained prepared horseradish
1   tablespoon (15 mL) light corn syrup
½   teaspoon (2 mL) prepared mustard
    Dash red pepper sauce
    Pinch salt

The sharp, piquant flavor of horseradish adds excitement to this yogurt sauce that goes well with cold sliced cooked chicken.

1. Blend all ingredients in 1-quart (1 L) saucepan; cook over low heat, stirring constantly, until hot but not boiling, about 3 minutes.

2. Cover sauce and refrigerate at least 30 minutes.

Spicy Applesauce

Makes about 2½ cups (675 mL)

1½ cups (375 mL) cold applesauce
½   cup (125 mL) whipping cream, whipped
1   tablespoon (15 mL) prepared horseradish, drained
¼   teaspoon (2 mL) ground cinnamon

This fluffy applesauce is a marvelous complement to either cold or hot poultry.

1. Blend all ingredients in small mixing bowl; transfer to glass serving bowl. Serve immediately.

Index

INDEX